A Century of Grace

A Meditation on a People of God in a House of God

St. Francis of Assisi Church

A Century of Grace

A Meditation on a People of God in a House of God

St. Francis of Assisi Church

PUBLISHERS DESIGN GROUP

Photography Copyrights
Pages xvi-1: Photo of Pope Benedict XVI by
Reuters/L'Osservatore Romano.
Page 2: Photo of Pope Benedict XVI by Reuters/Pool.
Page 3: Photo of Bishop William K. Weigand and of the 2004
Synod by Catholic Herald photographer Cathy Joyce.
Photo of Most Rev. Francis A. Quinn, Bishop Emeritus
by Catholic Herald Staff.
All other photos appearing in this book © 2008 by
Publishers Design Group, Inc. All Rights Reserved.

ISBN: 978-1929170-326
Library of Congress Control: 2008937003

Compiled by Fr. Anthony Garibaldi, O.F.M.
Edited by J.D. Warrick
Design and Production
Chuck Donald and Robert Brekke
Printed in China

PUBLISHERS DESIGN GROUP

P.O. Box 37, Roseville, CA 95678
www.publishersdesign.com
Marketing and publicity inquiries: 1.800.587.6666

We Adore You

(Adoramus Te)

WE ADORE YOU most holy Lord Jesus Christ,

here, and in all your churches throughout the world;

and we bless you,

because by your holy cross,

you have redeemed the world.

Contents

1

The People of God

IN ROME. Around the world. In Sacramento. At St. Francis. The people of God work and live and worship in, around, and among us. We are, each and every one of us, the people of God.

54

The House of God: The Home of the Sacraments

BETWEEN BAPTISM and death we come together as a community to partake in these "signs of Grace" (ccc1131) which were "...instituted by Christ" (ccc1131) and, uniting "the faithful with one another and binding them to Jesus Christ" (ccc950).

Foreword

"**THE LORD GIVE YOU PEACE!**" This greeting of St. Francis of Assisi surrounds you when you enter the church of St. Francis in Sacramento. People are brought together by God's grace as the "people of God." The focal point of the church is on the table of the Lord, where the Supper of the Lord is shared with all who come to receive. In the area of the original altar, the stained glass images of Abraham and Melchisedek remind us of the connection between our Jewish roots and the celebration of God's love through the sacrifice of God's only Son. Statues and images of Scriptural scenes, Franciscan Saints, martyrs, mystics, and holy men and women, offer the assurance that we are not alone, but surrounded by "a cloud of witnesses" (Hebrews 12:1) whose lives were driven by their love of Jesus. We may enter this church with our family, with friends, or perhaps we enter alone. But when we walk through the doors, we are joined by a community of the faithful and by those who have traveled through the centuries to be with us. Above all else, we enter into the house of a God of great compassion, who loves us and who blesses us through Jesus and the Holy Spirit. Enter this church with all your pains, troubles, sins, and heartaches. May you leave this church with courage, forgiveness, love, and peace.

Preface

THIS BOOK WAS UNDERTAKEN to commemorate the 100th Anniversary of St. Francis of Assisi Church in Sacramento, California. This house of worship, at 26th and K streets, is the second parish church to be built by the parishioners. The first parish church was built in 1895 at the corner of 25th and K streets in Sacramento, California.

The second reason for publishing this book is to permanently record the synthesis of spirituality and beauty as found in the architecture and decoration of this house of worship.

The third reason for this book is to point out to parishioners and visitors to St. Francis the symbolism and meaning that surrounds them both exteriorly and interiorly. Parishioners and visitors will come to appreciate and understand the tradition and heritage of the Catholic and Franciscan spirituality which surround them as they worship in this church.

The fourth reason for this book is to preserve and pass on to future generations the ways in which the spirit of the Second Vatican Council can be actualized in a living and breathing local parish. There is abundant and rich symbolism, meaning, and history in this building. To truly appreciate it, one must stop and look at what is there and reflect on the reason why it is there. We hope that this will be accomplished by this book.

This book is also a meditation on where we worship and how we worship. It will enhance our journey towards life with God, and help us to "connect the dots" both visually and intellectually in our search for God.

We are the parishioners and staff of St. Francis of Assisi Church in Sacramento, California. We are in the Diocese of Sacramento and the Franciscan Province of Saint Barbara.

We are a people of God in a house of God.

And all are welcome.

Acknowledgments

IN COMPILING A BOOK of this nature there are so many people who warrant acknowledgment and our gratitude for their insight, support and hard work. This book could not have been completed without hours and hours of time and talent from so many wonderful contributors.

St. Francis Church is not just stained glass and brick. Those are certainly elements, but the church is about the action of the Eucharist, and our first "thank you" must go to the parishioners. This is a diverse and vivid group of people who are full of the spirit of Our Lord, and without whose participation this book would have no center. During the development of this book, these good people allowed us to insert into their worship a group of photographers who documented many of our Feast Days. These good people, with a love for Jesus, and Francis and Clare, walk out of our doors carrying the Word of God with them into the world, and have allowed us to share with that world their participation in our worship.

The Staff at St. Francis must certainly be mentioned as well. It is their involvement that keeps the mechanics of the "business of the church" running, and brings rich insight into our liturgy and our worship practices. We must be sure to acknowledge the contributions by Fran Anderson, who worked tirelessly to lend whatever support was needed on this project and, as a result, was instrumental in so many areas. And to our Pastor, Fr. Anthony Garibaldi, O.F.M., who gave so generously of his treasure of time and talent to masterfully lead this project to completion.

Next there are the many, many people who labored on this project, which spanned nearly three years. We owe a thank you to them all, and would like to be sure to specifically mention:

Members of the Centennial Committee: Mike Falasco, Shaaron Gilson, Jennifer Stanley, John Berger, Gregg Campbell, J.D. Warrick, Rose Cartmill, Vickie Cosentino, Marianne Grisez, Richard Hernandez, Jackie Mikesell, Rosalie Rashid, Kay Skonieczny, Toni Tino, Diana Bosley, Judy Miranda, and David Sundquist, for his initial leadership of both the book project and the Centennial Committee.

As well as: Gormley's Funeral Home, Patrick Gormley, for allowing our use of a casket; Jerry Hollis, Truck Rental, for his assistance getting the lift into the church for photography; Publishers Design Group, for their management of this project and the design of this book; Richard Warrick, who provided use of photographic equipment; Kenan Osborne, O.F.M., for his composition of the Preface

And Robert Brekke, Billy Scanlan, Ed Asmus, and J.D. Warrick, for their stunning photography.

Introduction

IT IS THE CUSTOM OF FRANCISCANS throughout the world to say a little prayer when we enter a church. As you opened this book, you read that prayer, called the "We Adore You." May the Lord give you peace as you look through and mediate on this work, for this book is a record of prayer and beauty.

The cornerstone of the present St. Francis of Assisi Church was laid on October 13, 1908. The original St. Francis of Assisi Church was a wooden structure that was built on the corner of 25th and K streets. As the number of parishioners grew, it became apparent that a new structure had to be built to accommodate the number of parishioners who populated the surrounding area.

With permission of Bishop Grace, the second bishop of Sacramento, the Franciscan Friars began to build a new church. Since the friars belonged to the Sacred Heart Province headquartered in St. Louis, Missouri, they enlisted the talent of their provincial architect, Br. Adrian Wewer, O.F.M. Br. Adrian had already designed and built other churches on the West Coast, namely, St. Boniface, San Francisco; St. Joseph's, Los Angeles; St. Mary's, Phoenix; and St. Anthony's, San Francisco.

It was St. Francis of Assisi in Sacramento where Br. Adrian chose to combine the Spanish heritage of the Franciscan Missions with the German architecture of his cultural background. The exterior of St. Francis was formed in the mission style, while the interior reflects the German style. Br. Adrian chose as his model of Mission Architecture the Old Mission Santa Barbara. Thus St. Francis in Sacramento has two towers.

Br. Adrian was building a parish church according to the liturgical norms and traditions of the Council of Trent, which had placed the focus of liturgical worship on the Presence of Christ in the Eucharistic host. Therefore, the niche where the Eucharist was placed for Eucharistic exposition was the focal point of a church.

The Second Vatican Council placed its emphasis on the Eucharistic as an action, and therefore the altar at St. Francis has become the focal point of the church.

Being a Franciscan, Br. Adrian also filled the church with Franciscan spirituality as can be seen in the windows and the statues.

With the liturgical reforms of the Second Vatican Council (1962-1965), the pastors and parishioners of St. Francis adapted and renovated this sacred space to meet the new liturgical theology and to speak to their own spiritual needs as well.

In this building, Catholic history, Franciscan history, California history, and Sacramento history are all wrapped up together. St. Francis Church is a landmark for all of these histories. More importantly, in this building there are family histories,

(Continued on next page)

(Introduction continued)

individual histories, and spiritual journeys that were nourished, healed, and enhanced. Perhaps these human histories reflect the most important story about this sacred space.

In this book, we have attempted to "connect the dots" in the text by citing quotations from Sacred Scripture, since we believe that the Scripture reveals to us the manner in which we should live and worship. We have also cited quotations from the Second Vatican Council, since we believe that this Council was a gift of the Holy Spirit and a source of our inspiration for relevant and authentic worship in the 21st Century. We should be able to go into our past and retrieve what is good as well as look to the present and discern what will bring us closer to God.

There are many people who should be acknowledged for their time, efforts, and enthusiasm for our one-hundred-year celebration. Their names are listed in the Acknowledgments page. As pastor of St. Francis during this anniversary, I want to personally thank them for their contribution of time and talent.

Fr. Anthony Garibaldi, O.F.M.

The Church Throughout the World

FOR IN ONE Spirit we were all baptized into one body, whether Jews or Greeks, slaves or free persons, and we were all given to drink of one Spirit. Now the body is not a single part, but many.

—*I Corinthians 12:13-14*

1

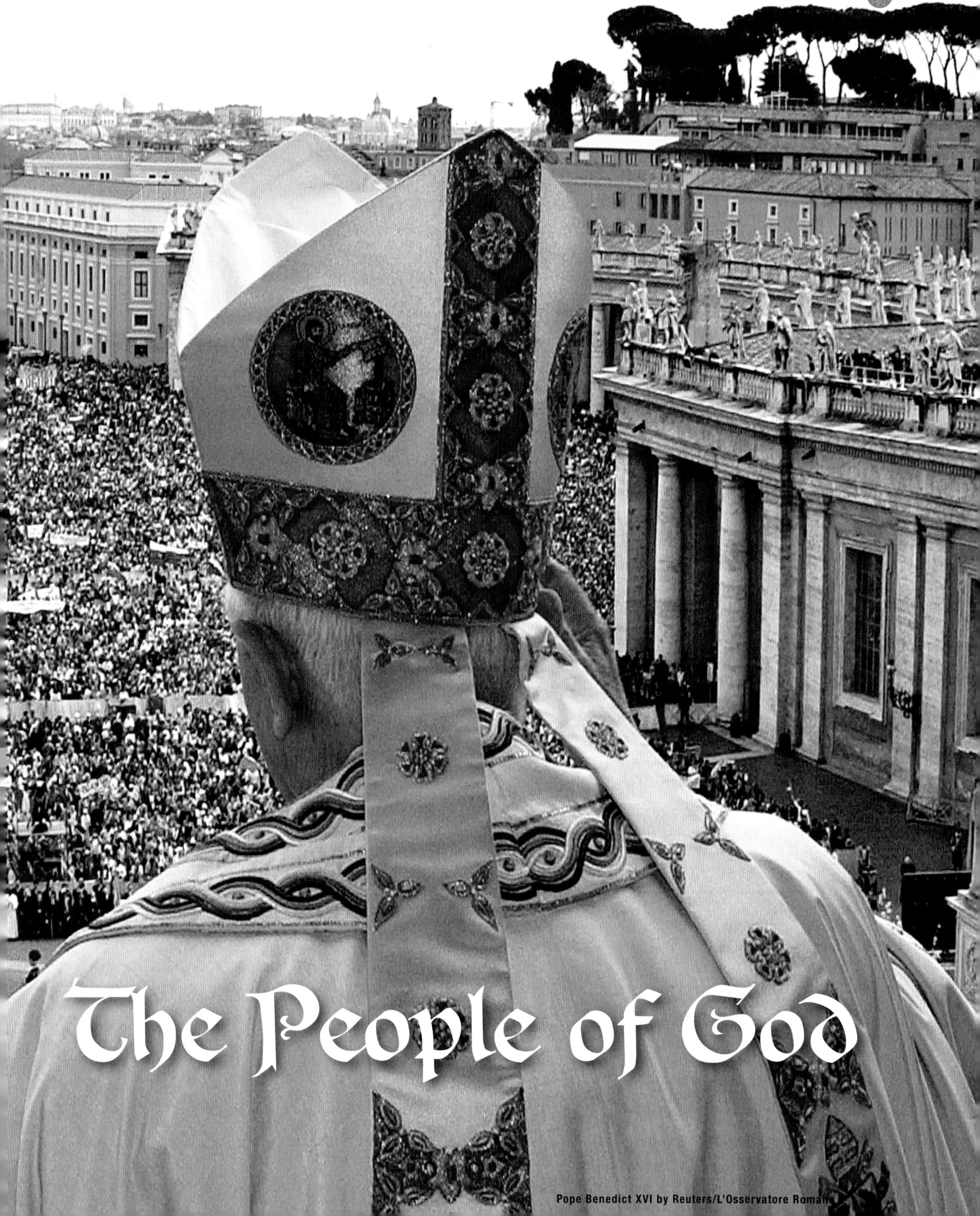

The People of God

Pope Benedict XVI by Reuters/L'Osservatore Romano

Pope Benedict XVI

He said to them, "Go into the whole world and proclaim the gospel to every creature."
—*Mark 16:15*

Papal Coat of Arms

Since the XIV Century, the two crossed keys have been the official insignia of the Holy See. The gold one, on the right, alludes to the power in the kingdom of the heavens, the silver one, on the left, indicates the spiritual authority of the papacy on earth. The mechanisms are turned up towards the heaven and the grips turned down, into the hands of the Vicar of Christ. The cord with the bows that unites the grips alludes to the bond between the two powers.
—*from Vatican documents*

Cathedral of the Blessed Sacrament

2004 Diocesan Synod

Bishop Jaime Soto

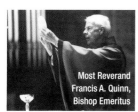

Most Reverend
Francis A. Quinn,
Bishop Emeritus

Most Reverand
William K. Weigand,
Bishop Emeritus

The Church
of Sacramento

BEHOLD, I STAND at the door and knock; if

anyone hears My voice and opens the door, I

will come in to him and will dine with him,

and he with Me.   *Revelation 3:20*

Metropolitan Bishop
Coat of Arms

This coat of arms is unidentified and
represents the Episcopacy.

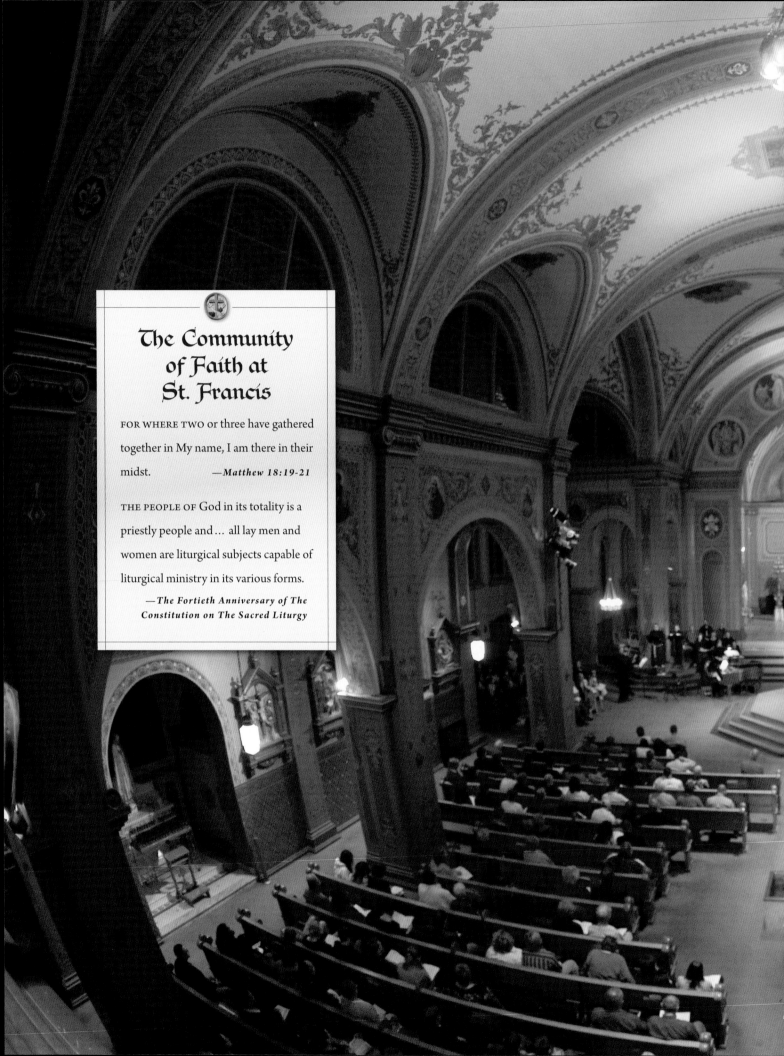

The Community of Faith at St. Francis

FOR WHERE TWO or three have gathered together in My name, I am there in their midst. —*Matthew 18:19-21*

THE PEOPLE OF God in its totality is a priestly people and ... all lay men and women are liturgical subjects capable of liturgical ministry in its various forms.

—*The Fortieth Anniversary of The Constitution on The Sacred Liturgy*

Weekend Mass: Saturday 5:15pm

Weekend Mass: Sunday 7:30am

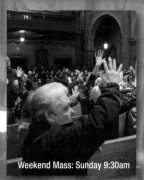

Weekend Mass: Sunday 9:30am

Weekend Mass: Sunday Noon

Weekday Mass: St. Clare's Chapel

Christmas Eve Family Mass

AND JOSEPH, TOO, went up from
Galilee, from the town of Nazareth, to
Judea, to the city of David that is called
Bethlehem…to be enrolled with Mary,
his betrothed, who was with child.
While they were there, the time came
for her to have her child, and she gave
birth to her firstborn son. She wrapped
Him in swaddling clothes and laid him
in a manger…. —*Luke 2:4a; 5–7a,b*

Christmas Eve
Family Mass
continued

When you fast, do not look
somber as the hypocrites do,
for they disfigure their faces to
show men they are fasting.
—*Matthew 6:16*

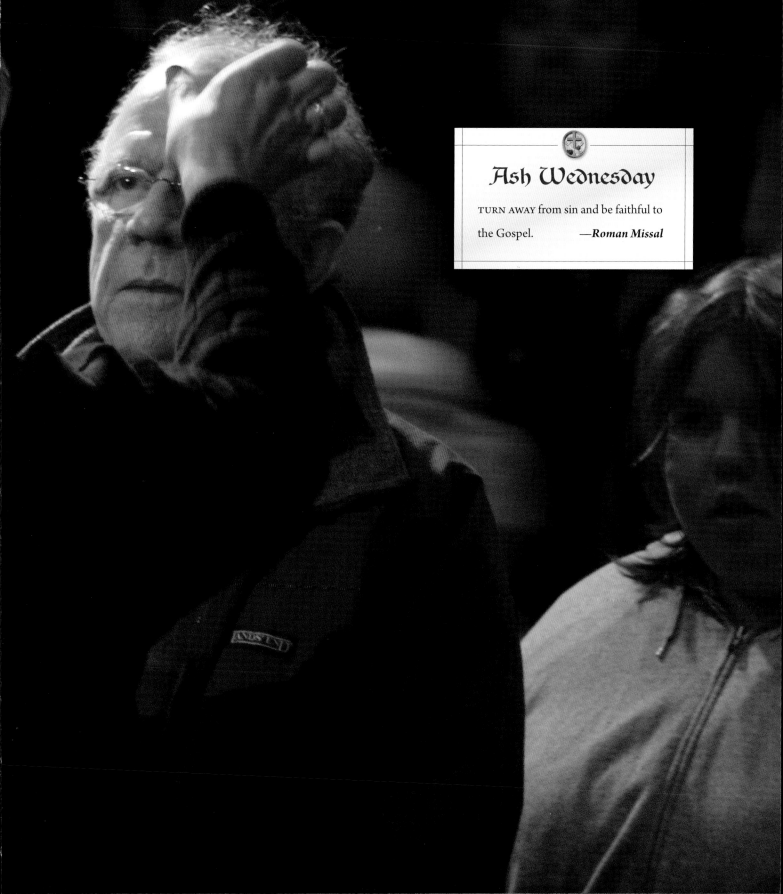

Ash Wednesday

TURN AWAY from sin and be faithful to
the Gospel. —*Roman Missal*

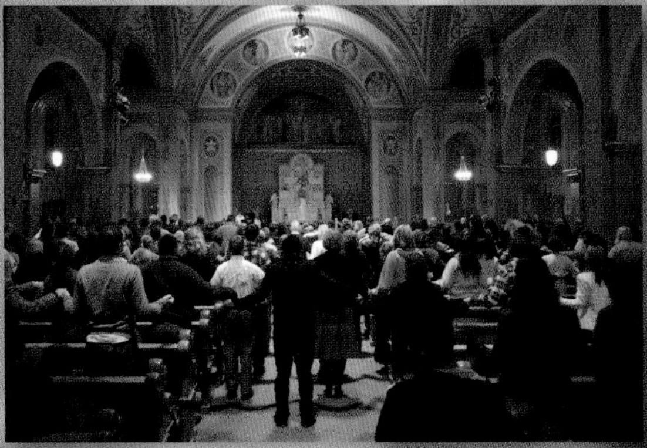

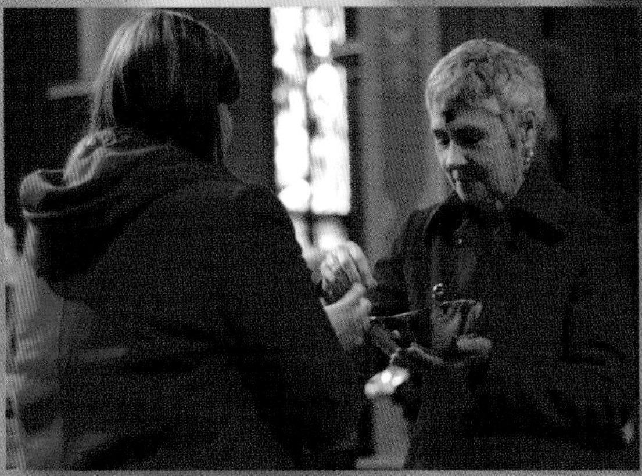

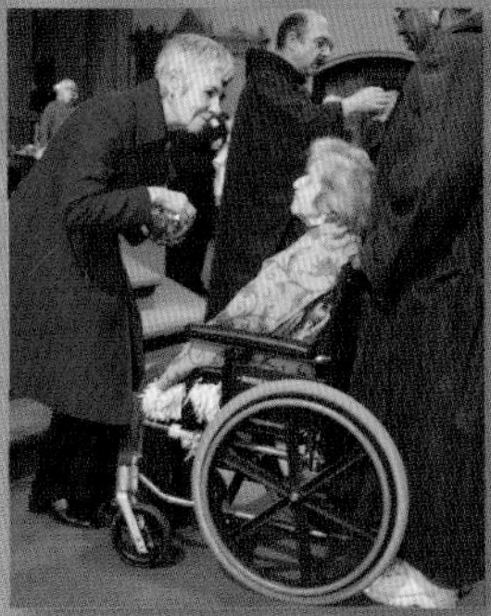

Palm Sunday

THE NEXT DAY the great crowd that had come to the festival heard that Jesus was coming to Jerusalem. So they took branches of palm trees and went out to meet him, shouting, "Hosanna! Blessed is the one who comes in the name of the Lord… "

—*John 12:12-14*

Palm Sunday

continued

Holy Thursday

WHILE THEY WERE eating, he took bread, said the blessing, broke it, and gave it to them, and said, "Take it; this is my body." Then he took a cup, gave thanks, and gave it to them, and they all drank from it. He said to them, "This is my blood of the covenant, which will be shed for many. Amen, I say to you, I shall not drink again the fruit of the vine until the day when I drink it new in the reign of God." —*Mark 14:22-25*

God of Eternal Blessing,
You have gathered us here
to share in the service and the supper
which were given to us by Christ.
We pray that in sharing and in living
this Eucharist we may grow more like Jesus,
your Beloved One, who lives and reigns with
you and the Holy Spirit,
one God, forever and ever.

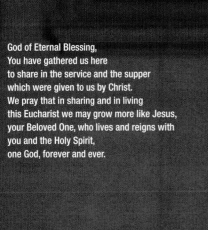

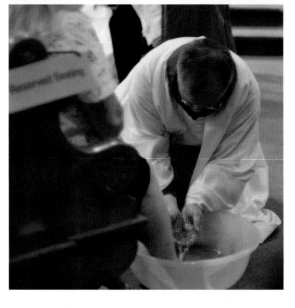

Jesus rose from supper and took off his outer garments. He took a towel and tied it around his waist. Then he poured water into a basin and began to wash the disciples' feet and to dry them with the towel around his waist.

Jesus came to Simon Peter, who said to him, "Teacher, are you going to wash my feet?" Jesus answered, "What I am doing, you do not understand now, but you will understand later."

Peter said to Jesus "You will never wash my feet." Jesus answered him, "Unless I wash you, you will have no inheritance with me." Peter replied, "Teacher, then not only my feet, but my hands and head as well."

Jesus said, "One who has bathed has no need except to have the feet washed, for that one is clean all over; so you are clean, but not all." For Jesus knew who would betray him; for this reason, he said, "Not all of you are clean."

When Jesus had washed their feet and put his garments back on and reclined at table again, he said to them, "Do you realize what I have done for you? You call me 'teacher' and 'master,' and rightly so, for indeed I am. If I, therefore, the master and the teacher, have washed your feet, you also should wash one another's feet. I have set you an example that you should do as I have done for you. I tell you the truth, no servant is greater than his master, nor is a messenger greater than the one who sent him. Now that you know these things, you will be blessed if you do them." —*John 13: 4-17*

Holy Thursday
continued

Good Friday

WHEN THEY CAME to the place called
the Skull, they crucified him and the
criminals there, one on his right, the
other on his left. [Then Jesus said, "Abba,
forgive them, they know not what they
do."] They divided his garments by
casting lots.   —*Luke 24:33-34*

The cross will come to
you. You cannot avoid it.
The cross will pass.
—*Robert Brekke*

My sisters and brothers, we gather today, the second day of our Triduum liturgy, to intercede with Christ and through Christ for those in need across the whole world,

🕯 to receive strength for the journey to the cross in the holy food of Christ's body,

🕯 to give, out of our generosity and gratefulness, in support of ministry in the Holy Land,

🕯 to listen to the readings from holy Scripture,

🕯 to solemnly remember Christ's passion and death,

🕯 and to venerate the cross, the symbol of Christ's overwhelming love for us.

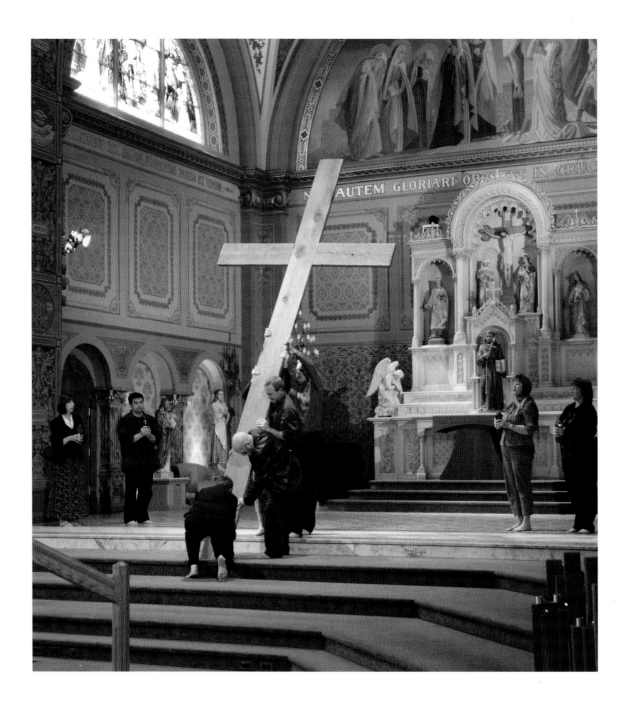

So, let us pray…

Holy God,
prostrate on the ground,
your Son prayed
that this cup be taken away.
But then he rose to do your will,
to stretch out his arms on the cross,
to be lifted up from the earth,
and to be glorified by you.

Open our hearts
to drink in the story of our salvation,
to stretch out our hands in prayer,
to venerate the cross
by which the whole world is lifted up
to salvation, life and resurrection.

We ask you this in the name of Jesus,
our Passover and our Peace,
now and forever.

Amen.

Easter Vigil

GOD OF FIRE and flame,
we shine with the light of
your glory through Jesus,
the light of the world.

Make this new fire holy
and inflame us with new hope.

Renew us by this Easter celebration
and bring us one day to the feast of
eternal light.

We ask this through Christ our Lord.

AMEN.

Easter Vigil
continued

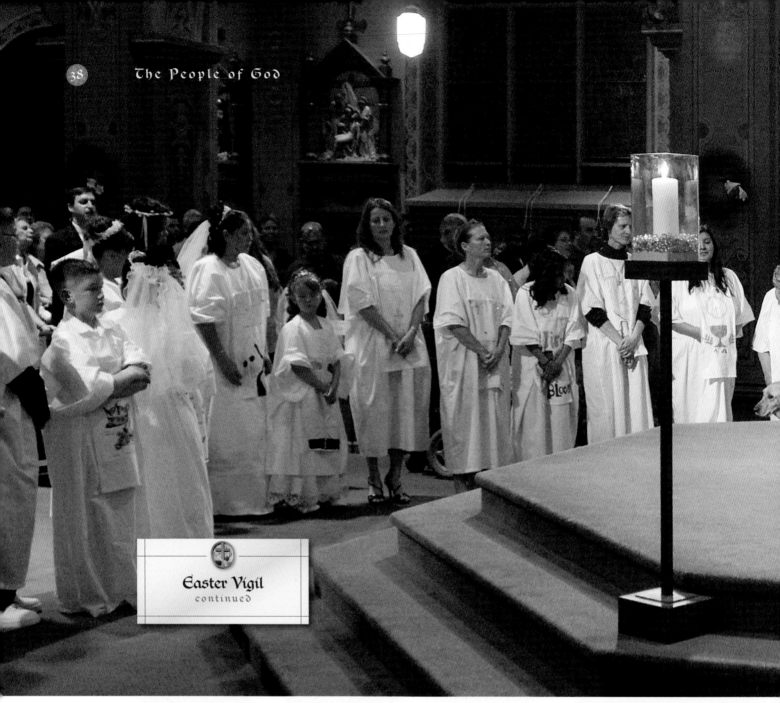

Easter Vigil
continued

Easter Sunday

ON THE FIRST DAY of the week, Mary of Magdala came to the tomb early in the morning, while it was still dark, and saw the stone removed from the tomb.

—*John 20:1*

God our Creator,
look upon us with love.
You redeem us
and make us your children in Christ.
Give us true freedom
and bring us to the inheritance you promised.

We ask this through our Lord Jesus Christ,
your Son,
who lives and reigns
with you and the Holy Spirit,
one God,
for ever and ever.

AMEN

Pentecost

WHEN THE TIME for Pentecost was fulfilled, they were all in one place together.   —*Acts 2:1*

God of wind and flame,
for fifty days we have celebrated the fullness
of the mystery of your revealed love.

See your people gathered in prayer,
open to receive the Spirit's flame.
May it come to rest in our hearts
and disperse the divisions of word and tongue.
With one voice and one song
may we praise your name in joy and thanksgiving.

Grant this through our Lord, Jesus Christ,
who lives and reigns
with you and the Holy Spirit,
one God, for ever and ever.

AMEN

Pentecost
continued

Pentecost
continued

The Friars

The Friar Community
From left to right: Fr. Anthony M. Garibaldi, O.F.M. (Pastor), Fr. Larry Dunphy, O.F.M. (Hospital and Jail Chaplain), Fr. Franklin Fong, O.F.M. (Justice and Peace Ministry), Br. James D. Swan, O.F.M. (Director of Music), Fr. Charles Talley, O.F.M. (Vocations Director)

> ## The Apostolate
>
> THE OTHER sacraments and all the apostolic works of Christ are bound up with, and directed to, the blessed Eucharist.
>
> —*The Code of Canon Law, 897*

For I was hungry and you gave me food, I was thirsty and you gave me drink, a stranger and you welcomed me, naked and you clothed me, ill and you cared for me, in prison and you visited me.
—*Matthew 25:35-36*

I want you to insist on these points, that those who have believed in God be careful to devote themselves to good works; these are excellent and beneficial to others.   —*Titus 3:8*

The most venerable sacrament is the blessed Eucharist, in which Christ the Lord himself is contained, offered and received, and by which the Church continually lives and grows. The eucharistic Sacrifice, the memorial of the death and resurrection of the Lord, in which the Sacrifice of the cross is forever perpetuated, is the summit and the source of all worship and Christian life. By means of it the unity of God's people is signified and brought about, and the building up of the body of Christ is perfected.
—*The Code of Canon Law, 897*

The Choirs of St. Francis

YOUR PROCESSION HAS come into view, O God,

the procession of my God and King into the sanctuary.

In front are the singers, after them the musicians;

with them are the maidens playing tambourines.

Praise God in the great congregation;

praise the LORD in the assembly of Israel.

Psalm 68:24-36

9:30am Sunday

The St. Francis Children's Choir

5:15pm Saturday

12:00 Sunday

7:30am Sunday

THE LITURGY IS the summit toward which the activity of the Church is directed (and) the font from which all her power flows. For the aim and object of apostolic works is that all who are made sons of God by faith and baptism should come together to praise God in the midst of His Church, to take part in the sacrifice, and to eat the Lord's supper.

—*Constitution on The Sacred Liturgy*
Sacrosanctum Concilium,
Solemnly Promulgated By
His Holiness Pope Paul VI

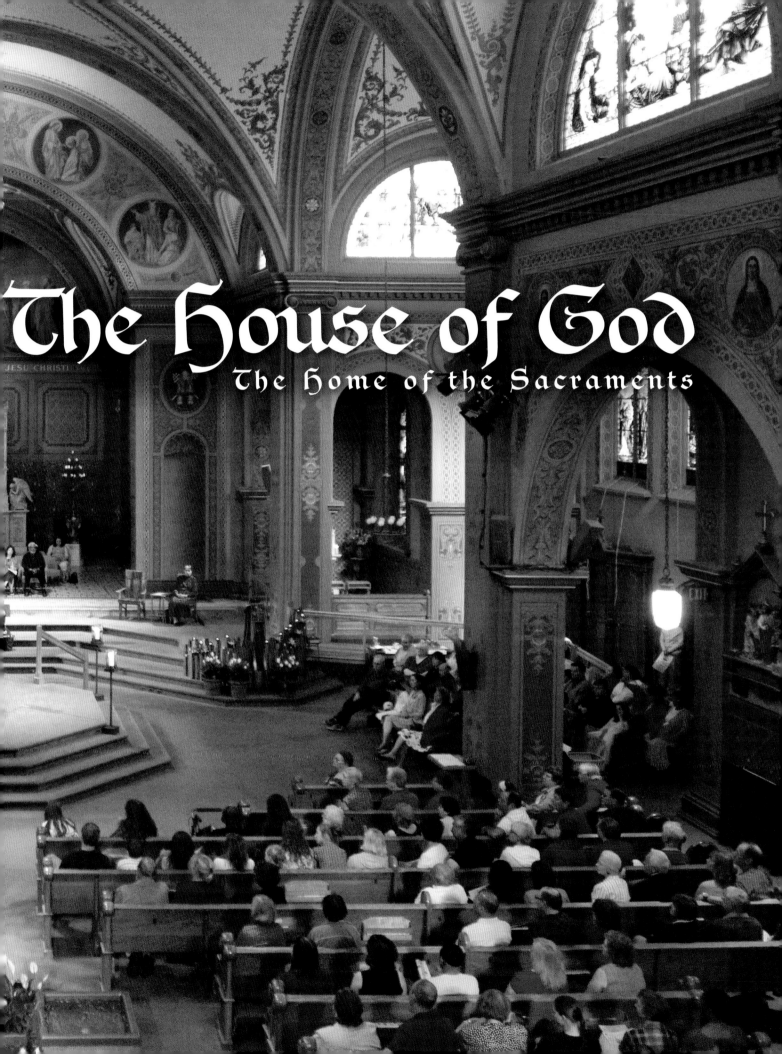

The House of God
The Home of the Sacraments

The Eucharist

THE TABLE OF the Lord

—*"Source and Summit"*

Arch Face:
Water Into Wine

The headwaiter tasted the water that had become wine...
—*John 2:9*

Arch Face:
Passover

It is the Passover of the LORD.
—*Exodus 12:11*

Arch Face:
The Last Supper

When the hour came, Jesus and
his apostles reclined at the table.
And he said to them, "I have
eagerly desired to eat this Passover
with you before I suffer."
—Luke 22:14

Arch Face:
Multiplication of Loaves

They all ate and were satisfied.
—Mark 6:42

Arch Face:
Manna / Moses

But Moses told them, "This is the bread
which the LORD has given you to eat."
—Exodus 16:13

The Eucharist
continued

The Liturgy of the Word

They devoted themselves to the apostles' teaching and to the fellowship, to the breaking of bread, and to prayer.

—Acts 2:41

Praise the LORD.

Praise God in his sanctuary; praise him in his mighty heavens....

Let everything that has breath praise the LORD.

Praise the LORD.

—Psalm 150:1,6

The Homily

The homily is an essential and required part of the Sunday liturgy, and an important element of any liturgy (Canon 767). A homily is given by a priest or deacon. It can be followed by a reflection by a layperson. Both are opportunities to look deeper into the readings of the day as they relate to the everyday life of the members of the community.

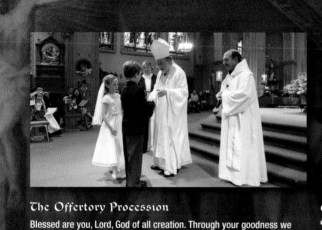

The Offertory Procession

Blessed are you, Lord, God of all creation. Through your goodness we have this bread to offer, which earth has given and human hands have made. It will become for us the bread of life.
Blessed be God forever.

Blessed are you, Lord, God of all creation. Through your goodness we have this wine to offer, fruit of the vine and work of human hands. It will become our spiritual drink.
Blessed be God forever.

Consecration of the Bread

Then he took the bread, said the blessing, broke it, and gave it to them, saying, "This is my body, which will be given for you; do this in memory of me."

—Luke 22:19

Consecration of the Wine

And likewise the cup after they had eaten, saying, "This cup is the new covenant in my blood, which will be shed for you."

—Luke 22:20

ORTE... IN CRUCE JESU CHRISTI : GAL 6

The Great Amen

Through Him, with Him, in Him, in the unity of the Holy Spirit, all Glory and Honor is yours almighty Father, forever and ever. Amen.

The Eucharist
continued

The "Our Father"

This is how you are to pray:
Our Father in Heaven,
hallowed be your name,
your kingdom come,
your will be done,
on earth as in heaven.
Give us today our daily bread,
and forgive us our debts,
as we forgive our debtors,
and do not subject us to the final test,
but deliver us from the evil one.

—Matthew 6:9-13

The Eucharist
continued

Communion
The Blood of Christ.
Amen.

Communion

The Body of Christ.
Amen.

First Communion

**Dismissal /
Recessional**

The Mass is ended, go in peace.

Mass of the
Resurrection
Christian burial

Whoever eats my flesh and drinks my blood has eternal life, and I will raise him up on the last day.
—*John 6:54*

NOS AUTEM GLORIARI OPORTET IN CRUCE JESU CHRISTI

The Altar of the New Sanctuary

EVERY DAY THEY DEVOTED themselves to meeting together in the temple area and to breaking bread in their homes. They ate their meals with exultation and sincerity of heart, praising God and enjoying favor with all the people. And every day the Lord added to their number those who were being saved.

—*Acts 2:46-47*

St. Paschal Baylon

Meditate well on this: Seek God above all things. It is right for you to seek God before and above everything else, because the majesty of God wishes you to receive what you ask for. This will also make you more ready to serve God and will enable you to love him more perfectly.

—St. Paschal

Window of St. Clare

By a happy coincidence the window of St. Claire and the medallion of St. Paschal adorn the area around the tabernacle. Both saints are known for their Eucharistic adoration.

The Tabernacle

For as often as you eat this bread and drink the cup, you proclaim the death of the Lord until he comes.

—1 Corinthians 11:26

Baptismal Font

ALL AUTHORITY IN heaven and on earth has been given to me. Therefore go, and make disciples of all nations, baptizing them in the name of the Father and of the Son and of the Holy Spirit, and teaching them to obey everything I have commanded you. And surely I am with you always, to the very end of the age.

—*Matthew 27:18-20*

Infant Baptism

Confirmation

The Conferral of the Spirit

...THEY SENT THEM Peter and John, who
went down and prayed for them, that
they might receive the Holy Spirit....

—*Acts 8:14b-15*

"Natalie, be sealed with
the Gift of the Holy Spirit."

Let us pray
that God will pour out the Holy Spirit
on our sisters and brothers.
All powerful God,
by water and the Holy Spirit
you freed your sons and daughters
from sin and gave them new life.
Send your Holy Spirit upon them,
to be their helper and guide.
Give them the Spirit of Wisdom
and Understanding,
the Spirit of Right Judgment and Courage,
the Spirit of Knowledge and Reverence.
Fill each of them with the Spirit of Wonder
and Awe in your presence.
We ask this through Christ our Lord.
AMEN

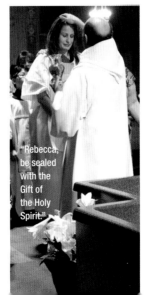

"Rebecca, be sealed with the Gift of the Holy Spirit."

Marriage

Put on then, as God's chosen ones, holy and beloved, heartfelt compassion, kindness, humility, gentleness, and patience, bearing with one another and forgiving one another, if one has a grievance against one another; as the Lord has forgiven you, so must you also do. And over these put on love, that is, the bond of perfection. And let the peace of Christ control your hearts, the peace into which you were also called in one body and be thankful. *—Colossians 3:12-15*

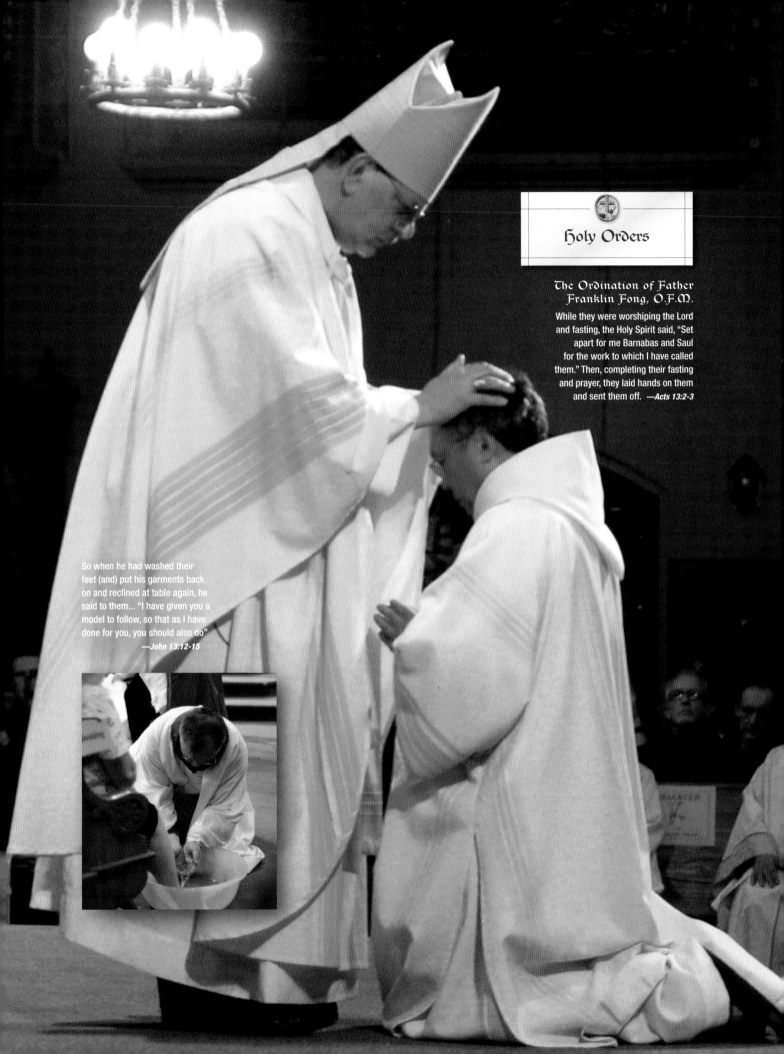

Holy Orders

The Ordination of Father Franklin Fong, O.F.M.

While they were worshiping the Lord and fasting, the Holy Spirit said, "Set apart for me Barnabas and Saul for the work to which I have called them." Then, completing their fasting and prayer, they laid hands on them and sent them off. —*Acts 13:2-3*

So when he had washed their feet (and) put his garments back on and reclined at table again, he said to them… "I have given you a model to follow, so that as I have done for you, you should also do" —*John 13:12-15*

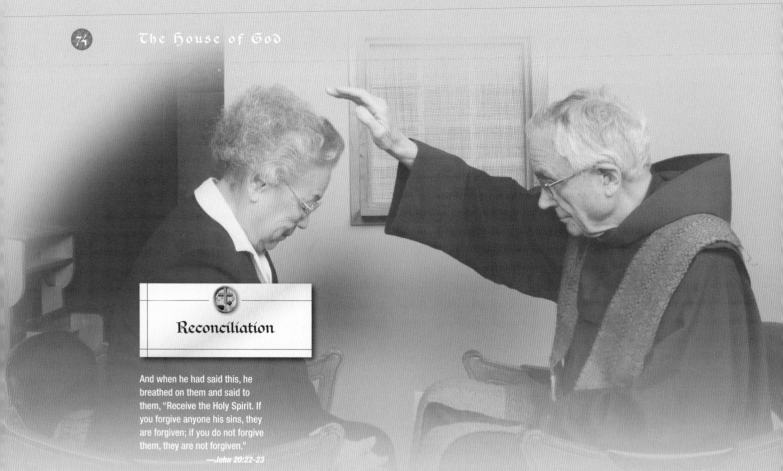

Reconciliation

And when he had said this, he breathed on them and said to them, "Receive the Holy Spirit. If you forgive anyone his sins, they are forgiven; if you do not forgive them, they are not forgiven."

—John 20:22-23

Used originally as the Baptistry, the windows of the reconciliation room represent baptismal images. We believe Reconciliation restores us to our baptismal status. The shell with water flowing from it is a symbol of baptism. The dove is a sign of the Holy Spirit, which is given at baptism. The lilies are a sign of purity and symbolize the washing away of sin at baptism. The snake, which tempted Adam and Eve in the Garden, is symbolic of original sin.

Anointing the Sick

Is anyone among you sick? He should summon the presbyters of the church, and they should pray over him and anoint (him) with oil in the name of the Lord.

—*James 5:14*

The Building

ADRIAN WEWER, O.F.M., (1836-1914), was a Brother-architect who entered the Franciscan Order in 1858 at Warendorf, Germany. He became the primary architect for the Franciscan Province of the Sacred Heart of Jesus—the "St. Louis-Chicago" Province—and served his Order in this capacity for half a century. The *Chronica of Santa Barbara Mission* estimates that he designed more than one hundred church buildings.

The designs of Brother Adrian were thoroughly imbued with elements of Neo-Romanesque or Neo-Gothic style—those styles typical for contemporary ecclesiastical structures in Brother Adrian's German homeland. He used three basic ground plan types for the churches he designed: the three-aisled basilica, the three-aisled hall church, and the wide hall church with no side aisles. To each of these three ground plan types he would sometimes add a transept. With few exceptions, the churches he designed have a flavor typical of medieval Germany. In California and Arizona, Brother Adrian exchanged standard elements of this Neo medieval style for characteristics of the Spanish Mission style.

Starting in June 1908, Brother Adrian spent most of his time in Sacramento, where, along with Brother Quirinus, he designed the St. Francis church building, which was constructed at the same time that the State Capitol was rebuilt. The contractors, "being German and thrifty," used the fine wood that was discarded from the Capitol for the stairway to the organ loft, the altar railing, and the base of the pulpit. The clever workmen transformed the gargoyles and animals into the heads and wings of angels. The stained glass was imported from Tyrol, and most of the statues came from Munich, Germany. Andrew Carnegie donated the organ.

On October 23, 1910, the new St. Francis Church was dedicated. The entire parish formed a procession in front of the residence of Bishop Thomas Grace, and with cross, banners, and band, proceeded to the church.

On December 23, 1913, Brother Adrian became ill. About six weeks later he was admitted to St. Joseph's Hospital in San Francisco, and it is there that he died on March 15, less than a month before his seventy-eighth birthday. He is buried in St. Mary Cemetery in Oakland, California.

—Sacred Heart Province Archives
http://www.thefriars.org/archives/items/adrian.htm

These windows of the Sacred Heart, which were placed over the side doors, are in the church because Br. Adrian Wewer, O.F.M., the architect of the building, as well as the friars in residence at the time, were all members of the Sacred Heart Province headquartered in St. Louis, Missouri.

Bl. Junipero Serra arrived in California in 1769, establishing a Franciscan presence that continues to the present day. The Franciscans ministered in the 21 California missions until 1823, gradually making way for the Mexican diocesan clergy (that is, secularization). In the late 1800s, the friars in California were placed under the jurisdiction of the Sacred Heart Province, founded by German friars and headquartered in St. Louis, Missouri. The Sacred Heart Province sent friars out to the West Coast to minister to German-speaking Catholics and accepted the responsibility to minister to the German and Irish Catholics of Sacramento, establishing St. Francis of Assisi Parish in 1894 and erecting a wooden church in 1895. The present church was erected in 1908 and dedicated in 1910.

St. Francis Parish and Sacramento, Snapshot: 1910

A parishioner arriving at the newly dedicated St. Francis church in the fall of 1910 may have walked or come by electric trolley. Both K Street and 26th Street had probably been paved by this time, but the church was still very much on the fringes of the city settlement. Across 26th Street stood Sutter's Fort. Among the tallest buildings in Sacramento were the six-story grain elevator and north silos of the Globe Mills at 12th and C Streets.

In 1910, the population of Sacramento was 44,696. Railroads were the largest employers, with canneries coming in second, as nearly all orchard fruit in California shipped through Sacramento. River steamboat lines carried a large share of passengers and produce to and from Sacramento. The business district was concentrated along J and K Streets, anchored on the east by the Cathedral at 11th and K.

In the first decade of the 20th century, Sacramento's population had become ethnically diverse, with large numbers of Italians, Portuguese, Croatians, Japanese, and Filipinos settling in to work on the railroads, the canneries, and the river lines.

The church bell was donated by Bishop Manogue following the demolition of St. Rose of Lima Church in downtown Sacramento. The bell, which is 46 inches in diameter, was cast in Meneeley's Foundry in West Troy, New York in 1859. After 36 years at St. Rose Church, the bell was moved to St. Francis Church and placed in a raised tower, where it rang for the first time at Bishop Manogue's funeral.

Midnight Easter Vigil, St. Francis

Entering
the Church

O GATES, LIFT high your heads,
Grow higher, ancient doors,
Let him enter, the king of glory!

—*Psalm 24*

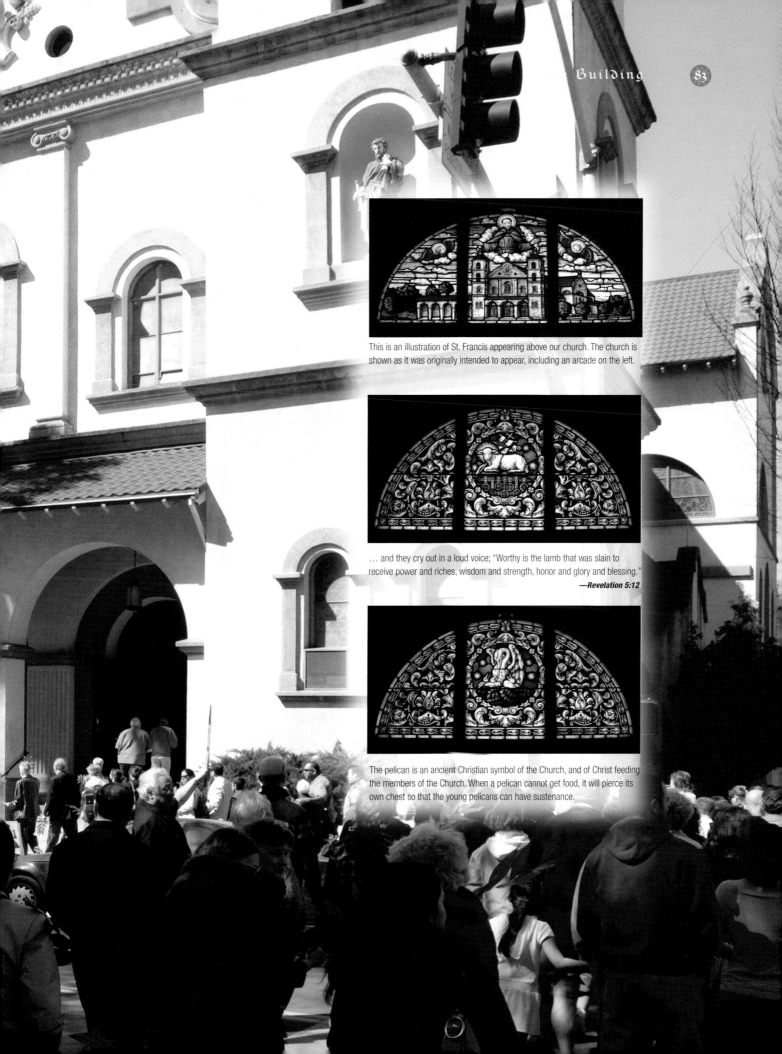

This is an illustration of St. Francis appearing above our church. The church is shown as it was originally intended to appear, including an arcade on the left.

… and they cry out in a loud voice; "Worthy is the lamb that was slain to receive power and riches, wisdom and strength, honor and glory and blessing."
—*Revelation 5:12*

The pelican is an ancient Christian symbol of the Church, and of Christ feeding the members of the Church. When a pelican cannot get food, it will pierce its own chest so that the young pelicans can have sustenance.

Old Sanctuary

The building was originally designed according to the liturgical norms and traditions of the Council of Trent, which had placed the focus of liturgical worship on the Presence of Christ in the Eucharistic host. Therefore, the niche where the Eucharist was placed for Eucharistic exposition was the focal point of most church buildings built after the Council of Trent.

There are five figures represented on the altar: Jesus, Mary, the Disciple whom Jesus loved, St. Louis of France, and St. Elizabeth of Hungary.

NOS AUTEM GLORIARI OPORTET IN CRUCE JES

Melchizedek Offering Bread and Wine

"Melchizedech Rex Salem Proferens Panen Et Vinum"
Melchizedek King of Salem offering bread and wine.

Then Melchizedek, King of Salem, brought out bread and wine. He was priest of God Most High, and he blessed Abram, saying, "Blessed be Abram by God Most High Creator of heaven and earth. And blessed be God Most High, who delivered your enemies into your hand." Then Abram gave him a tenth of everything.
—*Genesis 14:18-20*

The scene in this window is considered a prefiguration of the Eucharist in the offering of bread and wine. The priesthood can be traced back to the Order of Melchizedek. Because he has no recorded beginning and no end, Melchizedek prefigures Jesus.

It has been heard that you, Oh Lord, are in the midst of your people; You, Lord, who plainly reveal yourself! Your cloud stands over them, and you go before them by day in a column of cloud and by night in a column of fire.
—*Numbers 14:14b*

The Holy Trinity is visually represented above the area of the original altar in the form of the Seeing Eye of the Creator (Father), the Hand of Jesus (Son), and the Dove (the Holy Spirit). Placed high above the sanctuary space, these images are a reminder that the Trinity is present when the Eucharist is celebrated.

The Mural

"Nos Autem Gloriari Oportet in Cruce Jesu Christi"

But may I never boast except in the cross of our Lord Jesus Christ.

—Galatians 6:14a

Some women were watching from a distance. Among them were Mary Magdalene, Mary the mother of James the younger and of Joses, and Salome. In Galilee these women had followed him and cared for his needs. Many other women who had come up with him to Jerusalem were also there. **—Mark 17:40-41**

Many women were there, watching from a distance. They had followed Jesus from Galilee to care for his needs. Among them were Mary Magdalene, Mary the mother of James and Joses, and the mother of Zebedee's sons. **—Matthew 57:25-26**

The centurion, seeing what had happened, praised God and said, "Surely this was a righteous man." When all the people who had gathered to witness this sight saw what took place, they beat their breasts and went away. But all those who knew him, including the women who had followed him from Galilee, stood at a distance, watching these things.

—Luke 23:47-49

There they crucified him, and with him two others, one on either side, with Jesus in the middle. Near the cross of Jesus stood his mother, his mother's sister, Mary the wife of Clopas, and Mary Magdalene. When Jesus saw his mother there, and the disciple whom he loved standing nearby, he said to his mother, "Here is your son," and to the disciple, "Here is your mother." From that time on, this disciple took her into his home. When Jesus had taken the wine, he said, "It is finished." And bowing his head, he handed over the spirit. **—John 19:18,25-27,30**

After Jesus was baptized, he came up from the water and behold, the heavens were opened (for him), and he saw the Spirit of God descending like a dove (and) coming upon him.

—Matthew 3:16

In the New Testament, we see the dove as a symbol for the Holy Spirit. In the Eucharistic liturgy, the priest prays that the Holy Spirit will come down upon the bread and the wine and change them into the Body and Blood of Christ. Combined with the images of the Father and the Son on either side of the Old Sanctuary, together they remind us that we pray to the Father through the Son by the power of the Holy Spirit.

The Sacrifice of Isaac

"Extenditque (Abraham) Manum Et Arripuit Gladium"

Abraham extended his hand and the sword was seized. Some time later God tested Abraham. He said to him, "Abraham!" "Here I am," he replied. Then God said, "Take your son, your only son, Isaac, whom you love, and go to the region of Moriah. Sacrifice him there as a burnt offering on one of the mountains I will tell you about." Early the next morning Abraham got up and saddled his donkey. He took with him two of his servants and his son Isaac. **—Genesis 22**

The window is in the area of the Sanctuary because God gave us God's only son, Jesus Christ, who was sacrificed on the cross. Early Church theologians saw this as a prefiguration of the sacrifice at Calvary. In the section of the window on the right you will see a ram caught in the thickets. This prefigures the Lamb of God.

 ADORO

 QUAE

TE

SUB HIS

DEVOTE

FIGURIS

LATENS

VERE

DEITAS

LATITAS

Adoro Te Devote

1. Godhead here in hiding, whom I do adore,
Masked by these bare shadows, shape and nothing more,
See, Lord, at thy service low lies here a heart
Lost, all lost in wonder at the God thou art.

1. Adoro te devote, latens Deitas,
Quae sub his figuris vere latitas;
Tibi se cor meum totum subiicit,
Quia te contemplans, totum deficit.

The Primacy of Christ

Christ is the image of the unseen God and the firstborn of all creation, for in Christ were created all things in heaven and on earth: everything visible and invisible, Thrones, Dominations, Sovereignties, Powers—all things were created through Christ and for Christ. Before anything was created, Christ existed, and all things hold together in Christ. The church is the body; Christ is its head. Christ is the Beginning, the firstborn from the dead, and so Christ is first in every way. God wanted all perfection to be found in Christ, and all things to be reconciled to God through Christ—everything in heaven and everything on earth—when Christ made peace by dying on the cross. —Colossians 1:15–20

Jesus, Wedding at Cana

Jesus said to the servants, "Fill the jars with water"; so they filled them to the brim. Then he told them, "Now draw some out and take it to the master of the banquet." They did so, and the master of the banquet tasted the water that had been turned into wine. He did not realize where it had come from, though the servants who had drawn the water knew. This, the first of his miraculous signs, Jesus performed in Cana of Galilee. He thus revealed his glory, and his disciples put their faith in him.　　　　　　　**—John 2:7-9,11**

Jesus, Sermon on the Mount

Blessed are the poor in spirit, for theirs is the kingdom of heaven.
Blessed are those who mourn, for they will be comforted.
Blessed are the meek, for they will inherit the earth.
Blessed are those who hunger and thirst for righteousness,
　　for they will be filled.
Blessed are the merciful, for they will be shown mercy.
Blessed are the pure in heart, for they will see God.
Blessed are the peacemakers, for they will be called sons of God.
Blessed are those who are persecuted because of righteousness,
　　for theirs is the kingdom of heaven.　　　**—Matthew 5:3-10**

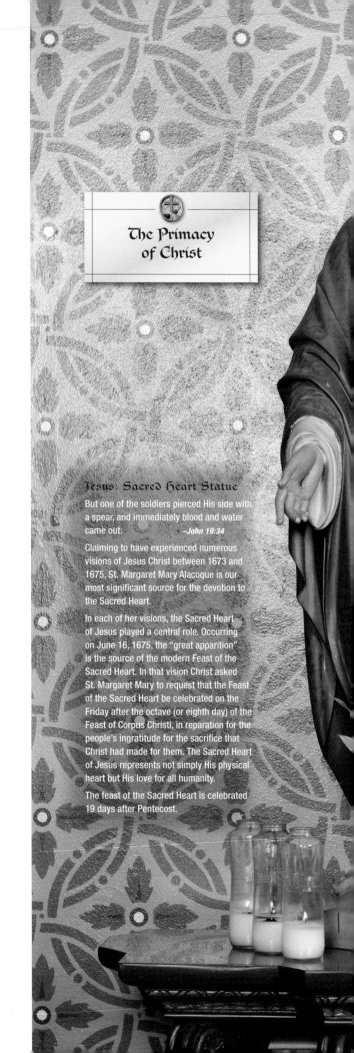

The Primacy of Christ

Jesus: Sacred Heart Statue

But one of the soldiers pierced His side with a spear, and immediately blood and water came out.　　　　　　　*–John 19:34*

Claiming to have experienced numerous visions of Jesus Christ between 1673 and 1675, St. Margaret Mary Alacoque is our most significant source for the devotion to the Sacred Heart.

In each of her visions, the Sacred Heart of Jesus played a central role. Occurring on June 16, 1675, the "great apparition" is the source of the modern Feast of the Sacred Heart. In that vision Christ asked St. Margaret Mary to request that the Feast of the Sacred Heart be celebrated on the Friday after the octave (or eighth day) of the Feast of Corpus Christi, in reparation for the people's ingratitude for the sacrifice that Christ had made for them. The Sacred Heart of Jesus represents not simply His physical heart but His love for all humanity.

The feast of the Sacred Heart is celebrated 19 days after Pentecost.

Jesus with the Children

But Jesus said, "Let the children alone, and do not hinder them from coming to Me; for the kingdom of heaven belongs to such as these."   —*Matthew 19:14*

Jesus, the Agony in the Garden

Then Jesus came with them to a place called Gethsemane, and said to His disciples, "Sit here while I go over there and pray." And He went a little beyond them, and fell on His face and prayed, saying, "My Father, if it is possible, let this cup pass from Me, yet not as I will, but as You will."   —*Matthew 26:36,39*

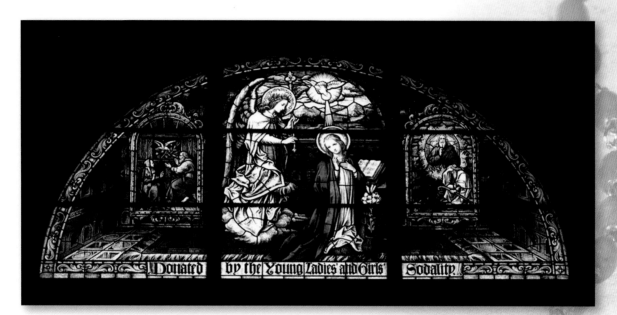

The Annunciation

In the sixth month, the angel Gabriel was sent from God to a town of Galilee called Nazareth, to a virgin betrothed to a man named Joseph, of the house of David, and the virgin's name was Mary. And coming to her, he said, "Hail, favored one! The Lord is with you."

—Luke 1:26-28

The Nativity

While they were there, the time came for her to have her child, and she gave birth to her firstborn son. She wrapped him in swaddling clothes and laid him in a manger, because there was no room for them in the inn.

—Luke 2:6-7

The Clerestory

THE WINDOWS OF the clerestory, when connected with the mural above the original altar, evoke the concept of the seven-decade Franciscan Rosary and offer an opportunity for individual reflection and contemplation. The Franciscan Rosary is also known as the Franciscan Crown.

Finding Jesus in the Temple

After three days they found him in the temple, sitting in the midst of the teachers, listening to them and asking them questions, and all who heard him were astounded at his understanding and his answers. *—Luke 2:46-47*

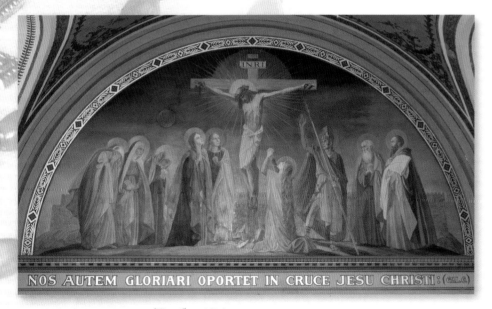

The Crucifixion

Standing by the cross of Jesus were his mother and his mother's sister, Mary the wife of Clopas, and Mary of Magdala. *—John 19:25b*

The Resurrection

After the sabbath, as the first day of the week was dawning, Mary Magdalene and the other Mary came to see the tomb. And behold, there was a great earthquake; for an angel of the Lord descended from heaven, approached, rolled back the stone, and sat upon it. His appearance was like lightning and his clothing was white as snow. The guards were shaken with fear of him and became like dead men. Then the angel said to the women in reply, "Do not be afraid! I know that you are seeking Jesus the crucified." —*Matthew 28:1-5*

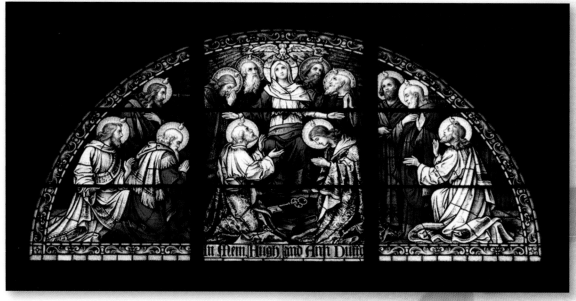

Pentecost

When the time for Pentecost was fulfilled, they were all in one place together. And suddenly there came from the sky a noise like a strong driving wind, and it filled the entire house in which they were. Then there appeared to them tongues as of fire…. —*Acts 2:1-3*

The Coronation

A great sign appeared in the sky, a woman clothed with the sun, with the moon under her feet, and on her head a crown of twelve stars.

—Revelation 12:1

The Clerestory
continued

Hail Mary, full of grace.

The Lord is with you.

Blessed are you among women,

and blessed is the fruit of your womb, Jesus.

Holy Mary, Mother of God,

pray for us sinners,

now and at the hour of our death.

AMEN.

This window represents the initials for Ave Maria.

The Stations of the Cross

ADORAMUS TE, Christe,
et benedicimus tibi.
Quia per sanctam crucem tuam
redemisti mundum.

WE ADORE YOU, oh Christ, and we
praise You, for by Your holy cross You
have redeemed the world.

**The First Station: Jesus is
condemned to death**
So Pilate, wishing to satisfy the crowd,
released Barabbas to them and, after he
had Jesus scourged, handed him over to
be crucified.   *—Mark 15:15*

**The Second Station: Jesus is
made to bear the cross**
… and carrying the cross himself he
went out to what is called the Place of
the Skull, in Hebrew, Golgotha.
                                    —John 19:17

**The Fourth Station: Jesus meets
His Blessed Mother**

**The Fifth Station: Simon helps
Jesus to carry the cross**
They pressed into service a passer-by,
Simon, a Cyrenian, who was coming in
from the country, the father of Alexan-
der and Rufus, to carry his cross.
                                    —Mark 15:21

**The Sixth Station: Veronica wipes
the face of Jesus**

The Third Station: Jesus falls the first time

The Seventh Station: Jesus falls the second time

The Eighth Station: Jesus comforts the weeping women

A large crowd of people followed Jesus, including many women who mourned and lamented him. Jesus turned to them and said, "Daughters of Jerusalem, do not weep for me; weep instead for yourselves and for your children …." —*Luke 23:27-28*

The Ninth Station: Jesus falls the third time

The Tenth Station: Jesus is stripped

When the soldiers had crucified Jesus, they took his clothes and divided them into four shares, a share for each soldier. They also took his tunic, but the tunic was seamless, woven in one piece from the top down. —*John 19:23*

The Twelfth Station: Jesus dies on the cross

And about three o'clock Jesus cried out in a loud voice, "Eli, Eli, lema sabachthani?" which means, "My God, my God, why have you forsaken me?" And when Jesus cried out again in a loud voice, he gave up his spirit. —*Matthew 27:46,50*

The Thirteenth Station: Jesus is taken down from the cross

When it was evening, there came a rich man from Arimathea named Joseph, who was himself a disciple of Jesus. He went to Pilate and asked for the body of Jesus; then Pilate ordered it to be handed over.

The Fourteenth Station: Jesus is laid in the tomb

They took the body of Jesus and bound it with burial cloths…. where he had been crucified there was a garden, and in the garden a new tomb, in which no one had yet been buried. So they laid Jesus there

The Eleventh Station: Jesus is nailed to the cross
When they came to the place called the Skull, there they crucified him, along with the criminals—one on his right, the other on his left. Jesus said, "Father, forgive them, for they do not know what they are doing."
—*Luke 23:33-34*

The Fifteenth Station: Jesus rises from the Dead
When the Sabbath was over, Mary Magdalene, Mary the mother of James, and Salome bought spices so that they might go to anoint Jesus' body. Very early on the first day of the week, just after sunrise, they were on their way to the tomb and they asked each other, "Who will roll the stone away from the entrance of the tomb?"

But when they looked up, they saw that the stone, which was very large, had been rolled away. As they entered the tomb, they saw a young man dressed in a white robe sitting on the right side, and they were alarmed.

"Don't be alarmed," he said. "You are looking for Jesus the Nazarene, who was crucified. He has risen! He is not here. See the place where they laid him. But go, tell his disciples and Peter, 'He is going ahead of you into Galilee. There you will see him, just as he told you.'"

Trembling and bewildered, the women went out and fled from the tomb. They said nothing to anyone, because they were afraid.
—*Mark 16:1-8*

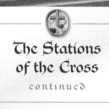

The Stations of the Cross
continued

ADORAMUS TE, Christe,
et benedicimus tibi.
Quia per sanctam crucem tuam
redemisti mundum.

WE ADORE YOU, oh Christ, and we
praise You, for by Your holy cross You
have redeemed the world.

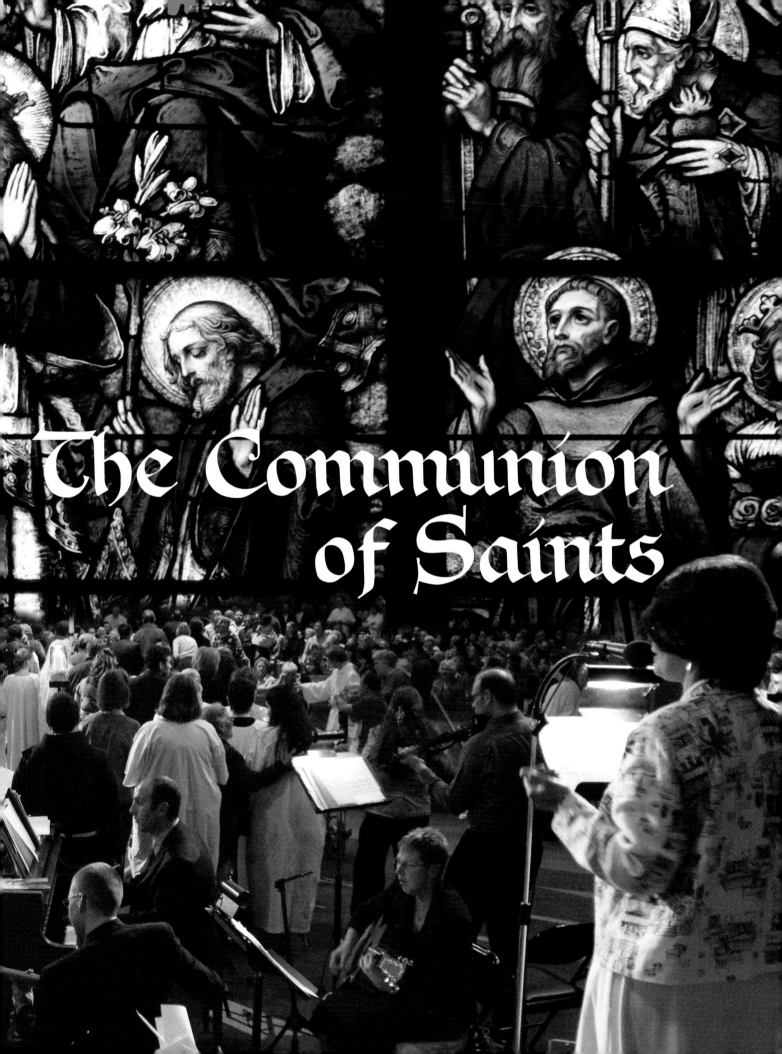

The Communion of Saints

MY GOD. MY ALL

St. Francis at Mt. LaVerna

While he was staying in that hermitage called La Verna,…he saw in the vision of God a man, having six wings like a Seraph, standing over him, arms extended and feet joined, affixed to a cross…. Signs of the nails began to appear on his hands and feet, just as he had seen them a little while earlier on the crucified man hovering over him… His right side was marked with an oblong scar, as if pierced with a lance, and this often dripped blood…. Sadly, only a few merited seeing the sacred wound in his side during the life of the crucified servant of the crucified Lord.

—*The Second Book of Thomas of Celano, Francis of Assisi, The Saint*

St. Clare and the Eucharist

In September 1236 hoards of Saracen mercenaries, the army of Frederick II, attacked the walls of the San Damiano monastery in the night as they made their way to the city of Assisi. St. Clare awoke to much shouting and noise. Having taken ill, she asked for assistance out of bed and proceeded to the small chapel adjacent to her room. There she retrieved the ciborium containing the Blessed Sacrament. Making her way to an open window where Saracens had already placed a ladder, St. Clare raised the Blessed Sacrament and soldiers who were about to enter the monastery fell away, while the others who were ready to follow took flight. St. Clare said, "O Lord, do not deliver over to beasts the souls that praise You! [Psalm 73]. Protect Your servants, for You have redeemed them by Your precious Blood."

The Franciscan
Men

A statue of St. Francis stands on the
altar in the original sanctuary. In his
hands Francis holds a book with the
Latin inscription *omnia et invenies
relinque, omnia* (When you give
up all, you receive all). Marks from
his stigmata are also evident on
his hands. When the Eucharist was
moved to the new tabernacle, the
statue of St. Francis was placed on
the altar to give prominence to the
patron of the Church.

St. Francis of Assisi

ST. FRANCIS (C.1181-1226) was the indulged son of Pietro Bernadone, a wealthy cloth merchant in Assisi. As a young man, Francis enjoyed raucous parties with his friends, then became a knight, fully outfitted by his father. On his way to battle, he heard a voice ask, "Is it better to serve the Master or the servant?" Francis responded, "The Master," and the voice told him to return to Assisi. Francis did so, though his courage was called into question. Subsequently, Francis joined up again, was captured and became a prisoner of war, became very sick, and when the prisoners were released at Christmas, he returned to Assisi and convalesced.

Recovered, Francis stopped at the Church of San Damiano near Assisi and experienced a vision in which the Cross spoke to him, saying "Go, rebuild my Church." Francis took this message literally, returned to Assisi, took precious fabrics from his father's shop and sold them, along with his horse. Pietro was furious and wanted his money back, appealing first to the city elders and then to the Bishop, who called on Francis to answer the charges against him. Before the Bishop and most of the city, Francis stripped himself of his clothes, returned them to his father, and said, from now on it is "Our Father who art in Heaven."

Francis began his work of rebuilding churches; after three years others began to join him. Francis received verbal approval from Innocent III in 1209 to live a life according to the gospel, without property, in chastity and obedience. On Palm Sunday, 1213, Francis accepted Clare Offreduccio into the Franciscan movement. She later became the first woman to write her own Rule of Life in the Western Church. Francis wrote a Rule of Life for lay people who wished to join the Franciscan Movement (the Secular Franciscan Order).

Francis inspired many, but humbly admitted that he was not a great administrator. He gave up leadership of the Franciscans and headed for the Middle East to become a martyr. The Sultan befriended Francis and gave him safe passage to the Holy Land, where Francis sought peace between the Crusaders and the Moslems. When Francis returned to Italy, there was great confusion among the Franciscan men concerning the Rule, so the Pope asked Francis to write a more formal rule. He wrote two; the Franciscan men thought the Rule of 1221 was too strict, so the Pope approved the Rule of 1223. Physically sick and nearly blind, Francis spent more and more time in prayer. In 1223, while on retreat at La Verna, Francis experienced the Seraphic vision that left him marked with the Stigmata, the nail prints and side wound of the Crucified. On October 3, 1226, Francis died at peace with God, humanity, and nature.

His feast day is October 4.

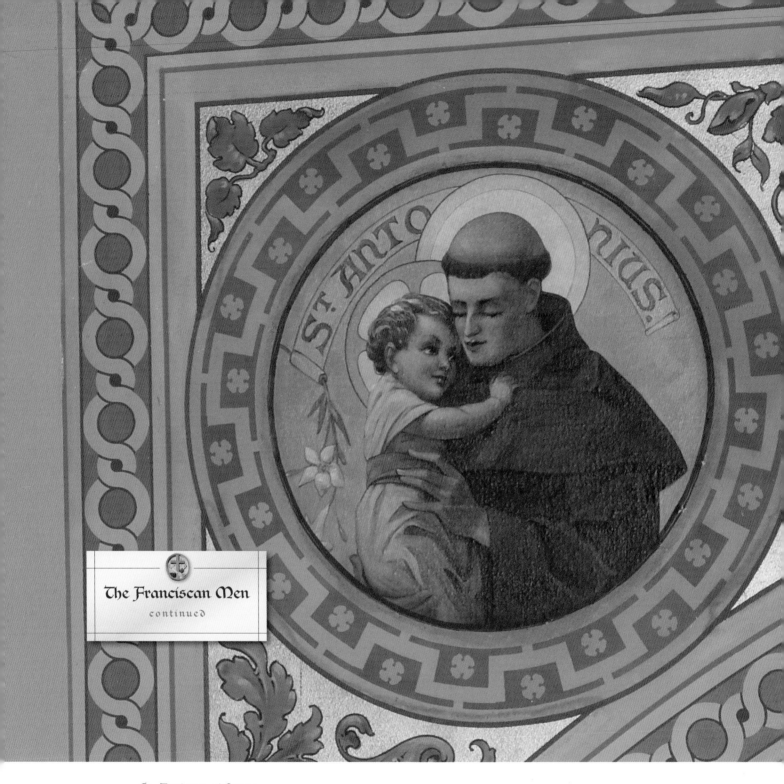

St. Anthony of Padua

Born in Portugal, St. Anthony, who was baptized with the name Ferdinand, first joined the Augustinians out of deference to his family. However, when Anthony witnessed the return of the bodies of the first Franciscan men who were martyred in North Africa, he joined the Franciscans in 1221, during the lifetime of St. Francis of Assisi.

Seeking martyrdom himself, Anthony sailed with others for North Africa. A storm arose and blew the ship off course, and it landed in Italy. Anthony then proceeded to Assisi, where he was present for the first Franciscan "Chapter of Mats" and where he met St. Francis. As the story goes, Francis assigned him to be a cook at a hermitage in northern Italy. Anthony obeyed.

While he was at the hermitage, an ordination was scheduled, yet no one was assigned to preach. As a joke, the guardian asked Anthony to preach. Anthony preached, and his gift for preaching was immediately recognized. He was sent to preach against the Albigensian heresy prevalent in southern France.

Francis gave Anthony written permission to teach theology to the friars.

After many years of preaching, Anthony died in Padua in 1231. His knowledge of the Scriptures earned him the title of *Evangelical Doctor* that was conferred on him by Pius XII in 1946.

In our church, St. Anthony is represented in the K-street side altar (See pages 136-137) as well as among the group of Franciscan men medallions.

His feast day is June 13.

St. Francis of Solano

St. Francis Solanus was born in Montilla, Spain, in 1549. He joined the Franciscan Order 20 years later in 1569. Francis Solano became a missionary to Peru in 1589. Francis had a gift for language and learned many of the languages of the indigenous peoples to whom he ministered. Francis Solano seems to have been able to address different linguistic groups using only one language, similar to the Pentecost miracle of tongues.

Francis Solano is most famous for playing the violin for his congregation. Thus Francis Solano is depicted in our medallion with a violin in his hands.

His feast day is July 24.

St. John Capistrano

St. John Capistrano was born in 1386 in the village of Capistrano. He studied law at the University of Perugia and was appointed governor of Perugia. While on a peace mission in 1416, John was imprisoned and had a conversion experience. Upon his release, John entered the Franciscan Order, studying under St. Bernadine of Siena. The two became life long friends.

Along with St. Bernadine, John promoted devotion to the Holy Name of Jesus. Both John and St. Bernadine, as well as a other friars, were accused of heresy and called to Rome, where John defended the group before the Inquisition. All the friars were exonerated. John also assisted Bernadine in one of the many reforms of the Franciscan Order and supported St. Collette in her reform of the Poor Clares.

At the age of 70, John was asked by Pope Calixtus V to preach and lead a Crusade against the Turks in Austria. John actually participated in the Battle of Belgrade, which ended that siege. He died of bubonic plague in 1456.

His feast day is October 23.

St. Bernadine of Siena

Born in 1380 in Tuscany, St. Bernadine was an eloquent and charismatic speaker who was also known as "Apostle of Italy." In 1402 he joined the Franciscan order, donating all of his possessions to the poor. For over 30 years, thousands of Italians attended his sermons, which sometimes lasted for as long as four hours. He died in 1444 and was canonized six years later.

His feast day is May 20.

St. Bernadine started the use of the symbol *IHS*, which symbolizes in Greek, *Jesus*, *Son*, and *Savior*.

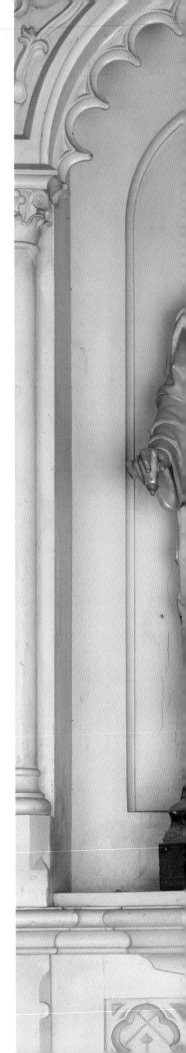

The Franciscan Men
continued

St. Leonard of Port Maurice

St. Leonard was a Franciscan proponent of the Blessed Sacrament, the devotion of the Sacred Heart, the Stations of the Cross, as well as the Immaculate Conception. He was born Leonard Casanova in Port Maurice, Porto Maurizio, Italy, and joined the Franciscans of the Strict Observance in 1697. Ordained in 1703, he began preaching all over the Tuscany region of Italy. By 1736 he was attracting huge crowds in Rome and elsewhere, and he erected almost 600 Stations of the Cross throughout the lands. In 1744, Leonard was sent by Pope Benedict XIV to preach on Corsica, returning to Rome in 1751 after receiving a summons from the pope. Leonard died at his friary, St. Bonaventure, on November 26. He was canonized in 1867 and named patron of parish missions.

"If the Lord at the moment of my death reproves me for being too kind

to sinners, I will answer, 'My dear Jesus, if it is a fault to be too kind to sinners, it is a fault I learned from you, for you never scolded anyone who came to you seeking mercy.'"
—*St. Leonard (Leonard Foley, O.F.M., St. Leonard of Port Maurice, pg. 9)*

His feast day is November 26.

St. Paschal Baylon

According to Butler's Lives of the Saints, in Spain the title of *Pascua* is given to other great feasts of the year besides Easter. Thus, Paschal Baylon earned his name by being born on Pentecost in 1540.

At 24 Paschal joined a Franciscan community. A humble doorkeeper for most of his life, he displayed a deep devotion to the Blessed Sacrament and the Holy Mother. It is quite fitting that his image adorns the wall of the alcove in which rests the tabernacle.

Many sources state that Paschal Baylon's spirit passed to

eternal life just as the bell was tolling to announce the consecration at a high Mass. For this reason, in 1897 Pope Leo XIII proclaimed him the patron of Eucharistic Congresses and fraternities of the Blessed Sacrament.

His feast day is May 17.

St. Bonaventure

St. Bonaventure was born at Bagnorea in Tuscany in 1221. He received the name of Bonaventure following an exclamation from St. Francis of Assisi, when, in response to pleading from the child's mother, St. Francis prayed for the young Bonaventure's recovery. Even though the child was ill when they first met, St. Francis could see something special was intended for the boy and is reported to have cried out, "O Buona ventura," which means, "O good fortune!" The boy recovered, and at age 22 he entered the Franciscan Order and was sent to Paris to study with respected doctors. It is here that he befriended St. Thomas Aquinas. At age 35, he became General of his Order, and it was during this time that he wrote his biography of the life of St. Francis.

His feast day is July 15.

St. Louis of France

St. Louis IX was a devout Catholic and was responsible for building the Sainte-Chapelle during the second half of the 13th century. Located in the center of Paris, the Sainte-Chapelle was constructed to house relics of the Passion of Christ. In 1239, St. Louis purchased Christ's crown of thorns from the Emperor of Constantinople. A few years later he acquired additional relics, including a fragment of the True Cross. Known for his charity, he fed beggars from his table, washed their feet, cared for lepers and the ill, and founded many hospitals. St. Louis is the Patron of the Secular Franciscan Order (SFO). The statue of St. Louis was previously located in the St. Anthony Shrine on the K-Street side of the church. It was moved to the altar to emphasize that Franciscan Life, living out the Gospel of Jesus Christ simply and humbly is not just for professed men and women, but can be lived out by the laity.

His feast day is August 25.

Bl. John XXIII

Born Angelo Giuseppe Roncalli in 1881, John XXIII was elected Pope on October 28, 1958. He was a member of the Secular Franciscan Order. Pope John XXIII is held with deep respect and affection in the living memory of many of our parishioners since he has become part of our spiritual living memory. John was elected because he was a holy and kind pastor who was expected to guide the Church along the usual path until he could be re- placed by a younger man. So it was with a great surprise that John XXIII convoked the twenty-first Ecumenical Council, know as Vatican II. A pastor at heart, John felt it was necessary to open the windows of the Church and let in some fresh air. He saw the

need to make the Church relevant to a modern world. As a result of his faith in the Spirit, the liturgy that we celebrate in this community of faith has its contemporary origin in John XXIII. John Paul II beatified John XXIII in 1993.

His feast day is October 11, the day Vatican II opened.

Second Vatican Council

The apostles and the presbyters met together to see about this matter. After much debate had taken place, Peter got up and said to them, "My brothers, you are well aware that from early days God made his choice among you that through my mouth the Gentiles would hear the word of the gospel and believe."

—Acts 15:6-7

St. Clare

CLARE WAS BORN in 1193 in Assisi, a small town in the Umbrian Valley of Italy. She was born from nobility, the oldest child of Ortulana and Favarone di Offreduccio. Civil struggle erupted between the nobility and groups of merchants and workers, and Claire, along with the women of her family, were sent to Perugia, where they lived as penitents with lives of prayer, fasting, and service to others.[1]

By 1205 they were able to return to Assisi, where Francis had already begun his personal conversion. By 1208, Francis had begun preaching, and a relative of Clare's became a follower. It is almost a certainty that Clare began to listen to Francis preach during this time. Being Called to God was a common, connecting focus in their lives.[1]

Attending a Lenten series of sermons preached by St. Francis at the church of San Giorgio in Assisi, the 18-year-old Clare became inspired by the words of St. Francis. On the night of Palm Sunday in the year 1213, this beautiful Italian woman stole down to the little chapel of the Portiuncula where Francis cut her hair and invested her with a thick veil and the rough tunic of the Franciscan Order. Thus Clare left behind the life of nobility to enter into the life of poverty. Having joined the Franciscan Order, but unable to live with a group of men, she went on to found the Order of the Poor Clares and become the first woman to write her own Rule of Life in the Western Church.

St. Francis wrote, "Because you have by divine inspiration made yourselves daughters and handmaids of the Most High, the Highest King, the Heavenly Father, and have betrothed yourselves to the Holy Spirit by choosing to live according to the perfection of the Holy Gospel: I want and promise that I and my friars will always exercise a diligent care and special solicitude for you as for them." [2]

Francis died at the young age of 45 in the year 1226. Clare lived on for another three decades, and struggled through illness and dissent in an effort to keep his ideal alive. Through service, she was able to be a reflection of God for others.

"May the Lord be with you always and, wherever you are, may you be with Him always. Amen" —*from the Prayer of St. Clare of Assisi*

St. Clare died in Assisi on August 11, 1253.

Her feast day is August 11.

---

[1] http://www.americancatholic.org/Messenger/Aug2003/Feature1.asp

[2] From "The Form of Living G iven to Saint Clare" (*Forn Viv*), by St. Francis

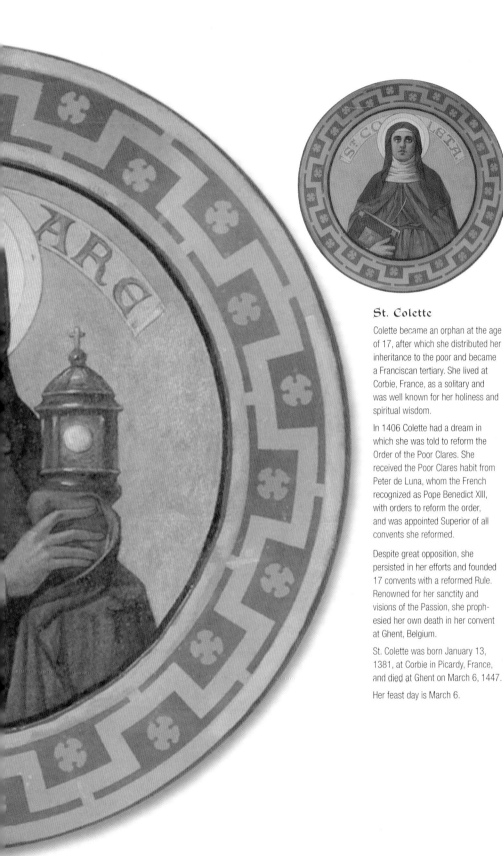

St. Colette

Colette became an orphan at the age of 17, after which she distributed her inheritance to the poor and became a Franciscan tertiary. She lived at Corbie, France, as a solitary and was well known for her holiness and spiritual wisdom.

In 1406 Colette had a dream in which she was told to reform the Order of the Poor Clares. She received the Poor Clares habit from Peter de Luna, whom the French recognized as Pope Benedict XIII, with orders to reform the order, and was appointed Superior of all convents she reformed.

Despite great opposition, she persisted in her efforts and founded 17 convents with a reformed Rule. Renowned for her sanctity and visions of the Passion, she proph-esied her own death in her convent at Ghent, Belgium.

St. Colette was born January 13, 1381, at Corbie in Picardy, France, and died at Ghent on March 6, 1447.

Her feast day is March 6.

The Franciscan Women

St. Veronica Giuliani

St. Veronica reportedly spoke her first words when, at the age of just a year and a half, she spotted a shop owner incorrectly measuring the oil he was selling. She told him to "do justice" and reminded him that "God sees you."[1]

At the age of 17, she was received into the convent of the Capuchin Poor Clares, where she took the name of Veronica, in memory of the Passion.[1]

At the age of 33, she received the impression of the Crown of Thorns, with wounds which were visible and painful for her throughout the rest of her life. The bishop ordered that she be given medical treatment, which was not successful.[1]

St. Veronica stated, "I felt a fearful agony of pain … but clearly saw and was conscious that … I had been thus wounded, in my heart, in my hands and feet."[2]

Veronica was canonized by Gregory XVI in 1839. She is usually rep-resented crowned with thorns and embracing the Cross.[1]

St. Veronica was born in 1660 in Merca-tello, and died on July 9, 1727.

Her feast day is July 10.

[1]Catholic Encyclopedia (http://www.catholicity.com/encyclopedia/v/veronica_guiliani,saint.html)

[2]Saints of the Day (http://www.saintpatrickdc.org/ss/0709.htm#vero)

The Franciscan Women
continued

St. Rose of Viterbo

St. Rose was born to a poor family in Viterbo, Italy, in 1235. At the age of three, Rose performed a miracle when she raised a maternal aunt from the dead.[1] At the age of eight, ill and near death herself, she was visited by the Holy Mother, who healed Rose and instructed her to enter the Third Order of St. Francis.

To those present, St. Rose stated, "All of you here, why do you not greet the Queen of the world? Do you not see Mary, the August Mother of my God, coming forward? Let us go to meet Her, and prostrate ourselves before Her majesty!"[2]

During this time German emperor Frederic II was in a battle against the pope. The Holy Mother also instructed Rose to "bring back the erring to the paths of salvation."[1] Years later, on December 5, 1250, Rose foretold the death of the emperor, who died eight days later.[1]

St. Rose died March 6, 1252, at the age of 18. Her feast day is September 4.

[1]Catholic Encyclopedia (http://www.catholicity. com/encyclopedia/v/veronica_guiliani,saint. html)

[2]http://www.magnificat.ca/cal/engl/09-04.htm

St. Mary Frances of the Five Wounds of Jesus

St. Mary Frances was born on March 25, 1715, into the home of a pious and loving mother and an angry and greedy father who worked her to near death. At age seven she received her First Holy Communion. At age 16, her father tried to force her to marry a rich young man, but she resisted, and instead, on September 8, 1731, she entered the Third Order of St. Francis, taking the name "Mary Frances of the Five Wounds of Jesus" out of devotion to the Blessed Virgin, St. Francis, and the Sacred Passion. St. Mary Frances received the Stigmata. Her charity and compassion, especially toward the afflicted and miserable, seemed to have no bounds. St. Mary Francis spent the last 38 years of her life in the house of a pious priest.[1]

St. Mary Francis of the Five Wounds of Jesus died October 6, 1791.

Her feast day is October 6.

[1]http://www.newadvent.org/cathen/09755a. htm

St. Elizabeth of Hungary

St. Elizabeth was the daughter of the King of Hungary, but spent most of her short life in Germany. At age four the young Elizabeth was brought to court in central Germany as the future bride of King Louis IV. Married at 14 and a widow at 20, Elizabeth chose a life of austerity and spent her few remaining years building hospitals and helping the poor. She died at the age of 24.[1]

St. Elizabeth is generally represented giving alms to the poor or as holding roses in her lap. According to legend, the bread she was trying to conceal turned in to roses when she was surprised by her husband, who asked what she was carrying in a pouch.[2] A contemporary of St. Louis of France, St. Elizabeth is noted for her charity and care for the poor and sick. "Often recall that you are the work of the hands of God and act accordingly, in such a way as to be eternally with Him." St. Elizabeth is the Patroness of the Secular Franciscan Order (SFO).

The Original Altar

The statue of St. Elizabeth on the original altar in the old Sanctuary was previously located in the St. Anthony Shrine. It was moved to the altar to emphasize that Franciscan Life, namely, "living out the Gospel of Jesus Christ" simply and humbly, is not just for professed men and women, but can be lived out by the laity.

St. Elizabeth of Hungary was born at Pressburg, Hungary, in 1207, and died at Marburg, Hesse, Germany, November 17, 1231.

Her feast day is November 17.

[1] *Wikipedia* (http://en.wikipedia.org/wiki/St._Elizabeth_of_Hungary)
[2] *Catholic Encyclopedia* (http://www.newadvent.org/cathen/05389a.htm)

St. Gregory the Great

Information about St. Gregory appears in the section titled "The Profession of St. Peter" on page 129.

His feast day is September 3.

St. Ambrose

When the Bishop of Milan died in about 374, there was division over who would replace him. St. Ambrose, a catechumen who had not yet been baptized, gave a passionate speech, not for one side or the other, but for peace. Suddenly a few spectators began to call out "Ambrose for bishop." Before long, it became many voices, and soon Ambrose became Bishop.[1]

Ambrose ranks with Augustine, Jerome, and Gregory the Great as one of the Latin Doctors of the Church.[2]

There is a legend that as an infant, a swarm of bees settled on his face while he lay in his cradle, leaving behind a drop of honey. His father considered this a sign of his future eloquence and honeyed tongue. For this reason, bees and beehives often appear in the saint's symbology.[2]

His feast day is December 7.

[1] http://www.catholic.org/saints/saint.php?saint_id=16
[2] http://en.wikipedia.org/wiki/Ambrose

Influential Thinkers of the Early Western Church

I CHARGE YOU in the presence of God and of Christ Jesus, who will judge the living and the dead, and by his appearing and his kingly power: proclaim the word; be persistent whether it is convenient or inconvenient; convince, reprimand, encourage through all patience and teaching. — *2 Timothy 4:1-2*

St. Jerome

St. Jerome was born about the year 342 at Stridonius, a small town at the head of the Adriatic, near the episcopal city of Aquileia.[1] He lived for years as a hermit in the Syrian deserts and was reported to have drawn a thorn from a lion's paw; the animal stayed loyally at his side for years. As Secretary to Pope Damascus I, Jerome was commissioned to translate the text of the Bible from Greek to Latin. The result of his 30 years of work was the Vulgate translation, which is still in use.[2]

His feast day is September 30.

[1]Catholic Online, Saints and Angels (http://www.catholic.org/saints/saint. php?saint_id=10)

[2]Catholic-Forum web site (http://www. catholic-forum.com/

Other Saints

St. Godfrey of Merville

In some catalogs of Catholic Saints you may find two different saints named Godfrey. Both lived at the same time and both were martyred by the Calvinists in 1752 at Gorkum. But Godfey of Merville was a member of the Franciscan household in Gorkum.[1] He was one of nineteen who were hanged on July 9, 1572, for loyalty to the pope and their belief in the Real Presence in the Eucharist.[2]

His feast day is July 9.

[1]http://www.catholic.org/saints/saint. php?saint_id=395

[2]https://www.sqpn.com/martyr17.htm

St. Augustine

Augustine of Hippo (354-430) envisioned a form of religious community life in which the members would "live in harmony, being united in mind and heart on the way to God." He wrote a Rule outlining the basic principles of this sort of life. Today Augustinians and many other religious orders and congregations still use this Rule as their guide. As Bishop, Augustine ministered to the spiritual and material needs of his people. He wrote extensively. We have today a vast collection of his writing: 113 books, 207 letters, and more than 500 sermons. His most famous works are *The Confessions*, *City of God*, and *The Trinity*.[1]

His feast day is August 28.

[1]Order of St. Augustine Web site, Saints section (http://osanet.fasthosting.it/en/ default.htm)

St. Adrian of Nicomedia

St. Adrian was, according to legend, a pagan officer and bodyguard for the imperial court of Nicomedia. Assigned to the horrific task of torturing Christians, Adrian was moved by their courage and strength. One account has St. Adrian asking a group of Christians what reward they expected for their suffering, to which they replied, "No eye has seen, no ear has heard, no mind has conceived what God has prepared for those who love him—but God has revealed it to us by his Spirit." (1 Corinthians 2:9) So moved was he that he at once declared himself a Christian. He was imprisoned and suffered torture before his execution on March 3 in the year 303 or 304.

St. Adrian is the Patron Saint of the architect of our church, Br. Adrian Wewer, O.F.M.

His feast day is September 8.

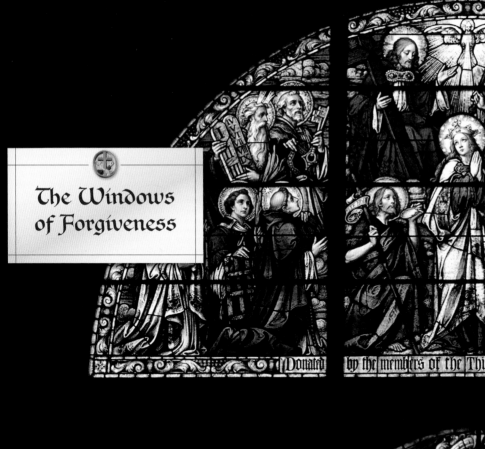

The Windows
of Forgiveness

Donated by the members of the Third Order of St. Francis of Assisi.

The Prodigal Son

A man had two sons, and the younger son said to his father, "Father, give me the share of your estate that should come to me." So the father divided the property between them. After a few days, the younger son collected all his belongings and set off to a distant country where he squandered his inheritance on a life of dissipation.

When he had freely spent everything, a severe famine struck that country, and he found himself in dire need. So he hired himself out to one of the local citizens who sent him to his farm to tend the swine. And he longed to eat his fill of the pods on which the swine fed, but nobody gave him any.

Coming to his senses he thought, "How many of my father's hired workers have more than enough food to eat, but here am I, dying from hunger. I shall get up and go to my father and I shall say to him, 'Father, I have sinned against heaven and against you. I no longer deserve to be called your son; treat me as you would treat one of your hired workers.'"

So he got up and went back to his father. While he was still a long way off, his father caught sight of him, and was filled with compassion. He ran to his son, embraced him and kissed him. His son said to him, "Father, I have sinned against heaven and against you; I no longer deserve to be called your son."

But his father ordered his servants, "Quickly bring the finest robe and put it on him; put a ring on his finger and sandals on his feet. Take the fattened calf and slaughter it. Then let us celebrate with a feast, because this son of mine was dead, and has come to life again; he was lost, and has been found." Then the celebration began.

Now the older son had been out in the field and, on his way back, as he neared the house, he heard the sound of music and dancing. He called one of the servants and asked what this might mean. The servant said to him, "Your brother has returned and your father has slaughtered the fattened calf because he has him back safe and sound."

He became angry, and when he refused to enter the house, his father came out and pleaded with him. He said to his father in reply, "Look, all these years I served you and not once did I disobey your orders; yet you never gave me even a young goat to feast on with my friends. But when your son returns who swallowed up your property with prostitutes, for him you slaughter the fattened calf."

He said to him, "My son, you are here with me always; everything I have is yours. But now we must celebrate and rejoice, because your brother was dead and has come to life again; he was lost and has been found." —*Luke 15:11-32*

St. Peter

Then the maid who was the gatekeeper said to Peter, "You are not one of this man's disciples, are you?" He said, "I am not…." Now Simon Peter was standing there keeping warm. And they said to him, "You are not one of his disciples, are you?" He denied it and said, "I am not." One of the slaves of the high priest, a relative of the one whose ear Peter had cut off, said, "Didn't I see you in the garden with him?" Again Peter denied it. And immediately the cock crowed.

—*John 18:17,25-27*

John the Baptist

John (the) Baptist appeared in the desert proclaiming a baptism of repentance for the forgiveness of sins…. John was clothed in camel's hair, with a leather belt around his waist. He fed on locusts and wild honey. And this is what he proclaimed: "One mightier than I is coming after me. I am not worthy to stoop and loosen the thongs of his sandals. I have baptized you with water; he will baptize you with the Holy Spirit."

—*Mark 1:4,6-8*

Mary Magdalene

Afterward he journeyed from one town and village to another, preaching and proclaiming the good news of the kingdom of God. Accompanying him were the Twelve and some women who had been cured of evil spirits and infirmities, Mary, called Magdalene, from whom seven demons had gone out, Joanna, the wife of Herod's steward Chuza, Susanna, and many others who provided for them out of their resources. —*Luke 8:1-3*

Mary Magdalene became one of Christ's true friends after He touched her life. She is most likely the woman with the alabaster jar who recognized Christ's majesty and so anointed Him and washed His feet with her hair. At the crucifixion, Magdalene loyally remained at the foot of the cross, alongside Our Lady and St. John. Finally, upon His resurrection, it was to Mary Magdalene Christ appeared first, even before Simon Peter.

As in many other images of Mary Magdalene, this window depicts her holding a skull, symbol of penitence and the contemplative life, with the jar of oil at her feet.

Margaret of Cortona

Her mother died when St. Margaret was only seven, leaving her with a cruel father and uncaring stepmother. She eventually escaped by eloping with a young nobleman, with whom she lived out of wedlock for nine years. After bearing him a son, Margaret begged him to marry her, but he never did. According to legend, after Margaret and he spent a passionate night together, he awoke the next morning, rode into the forest, and was murdered. His dog returned to Margaret and barked until she followed it to his body. In our window, Margaret is shown with the dog at her feet.

His death led to St. Margaret's conversion to Christianity. Homeless and rejected by her father, Margaret and her tiny son took shelter with the Friars minor at Cortona. After much soul searching and spiritual direction from the friars, Margaret became a Franciscan tertiary in 1277 and sent her son to school, where he remained until he entered the Franciscan Order. St. Margaret developed a tremendous devotion to the Eucharist and Passion, becoming so prayerful that she had a vision of Christ. In 1286, Margaret established a hospital for the poor of Cortona, staffed by Franciscan nursing sisters whom she named the *Poverelle* (Poor Ones).[1]

[1] *Butler's Lives of the Saints*, pp.54-56; www.catholic-forum.com/
saints/saintm27.htm

Left Pane

Moses, holding the Ten Commandments

St. Peter, holding two keys

St. Agnes, holding a lamb

St. Lawrence, with the gridiron upon which he was martyred

St. Dominic, with Rosary

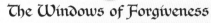

AFTER THIS I HAD a vision of a great multitude, which no one could count, from every nation, race, people, and tongue. They stood before the throne and before the Lamb, wearing white robes and holding palm branches in their hands. They cried out in a loud voice: "Salvation comes from our God, who is seated on the throne, and from the Lamb." —*Revelation 7: 9-10*

Center Pane

Jesus, with the cross

The Holy Spirit, represented by a dove

God the Father, with triangle halo because He is the Maker of heaven and earth

John the Baptist

Mary, who is the first saint and is in the center

St. Joseph

Right Pane

St. Paul

St. Augustine, holding a burning heart. He says: "Our hearts are restless until they rest in Thee."

St. Francis of Assisi

St. Elizabeth of Hungary

St. Ignatius

In loving mem. of John Meister

The Last Judgment

At the appointed time the Promised One will come in glory, escorted by all the angels of heaven, and will sit upon the royal throne, with all the nations assembled below. Then the Promised One will separate them from one another, as a shepherd divides the sheep from the goats. The sheep will be placed on the right hand, the goats on the left. —*Matthew 25:31-33*

The Profession
of St. Peter
continued

The Profession of St. Peter

Jesus said to him in reply, "Blessed are you, Simon son of Jonah. For flesh and blood has not revealed this to you, but my heavenly Father. And so I say to you, you are Peter, and upon this rock I will build my church, and the gates of the netherworld shall not prevail against it. I will give you the keys to the kingdom of heaven. Whatever you bind on earth shall be bound in heaven; and whatever you loose on earth shall be loosed in heaven."

—*Matthew 16:17-19*

St. Boniface, Apostle of Germany

St. Boniface, the "Apostle of the Germans," was born c.673-680 in Crediton, Devonshire, in England. He was a missionary who propagated Christianity in the Frankish Empire during the 8th century.

He was martyred in Frisia in 754: "… [A] group of armed inhabitants… slew the aged archbishop. According to their own law (the *Lex Frisionum*), the Frisians had the right to kill him, since he had destroyed their shrines. Boniface's hagiographer reports that the Frisians killed the saint because they believed the chests he carried with him contained gold and other riches, but were dismayed to discover only the bishop's books."[1] Our church window shows St. Boniface holding a book pierced by a sword, showing how and why he was martyred. He is the Patron Saint of Germany and the Netherlands. His tomb is in the crypt of Fulda Cathedral in Germany.

His feast day is October 5.

[1]http://en.wikipedia.org/wiki/St._Boniface

St. Gregory VII or Gregory VIII

Parish documents suggest that this could be a representation of either Pope Gregory VII or Pope Gregory VIII.

Gregory VIII (c. 1100-1187) died after serving just 57 days as pontiff. His first act as pope was to call for the Third Crusade; little else was accomplished during his short papacy.

On the other hand, Pope Gregory VII has been called one of the greatest of the Roman pontiffs and one of the most remarkable men of all times. Gregory was exiled to Germany with Gregory VI, and was closely tied to, and often at odds with, Emperor Henry IV.

St. Gregory was responsible for establishing a decree of election, whereby the power of choosing the pope was given to the College of Cardinals.

The feast day of St. Gregory VII is May 25.

Sources: Wikipedia, Catholic Encyclopedia, Catholic-forum.org, catholic.org

Pope Gregory the Great, Pope and Doctor of the Church

A system of writing down reminders of chant melodies was probably devised by monks around 800 to aid in unifying the church service throughout the Frankish Empire. Charlemagne brought cantors from the papal chapel in Rome to instruct his clerics in the "authentic" liturgy. A program of propaganda spread the idea that the chant used in Rome came directly from Gregory the Great, who had died two centuries earlier and was universally venerated. Pictures were made to depict the dove of the Holy Spirit perched on Gregory's shoulder, singing God's authentic form of chant into his ear. This gave rise to calling the music "Gregorian chant." A more accurate term is "plainsong" or "plainchant."

When Augustine asked whether to use Roman or Gallican customs in the Mass in England, Gregory said, in effect, whatever advances the Faith, for "...things are not to be loved for the sake of a place, but places are to be loved for the sake of their good things." (Bede, *Ecclesiastical History*, i 27 III, ed. McClure, Collins, Oxford 1994).

His feast day is September 3.

Sources: Wikipedia, Catholic.org

St. Patrick

Kidnapped from the British mainland at around age 16, Patrick was shipped to Ireland as a slave. Sent to the mountains as a shepherd, he spent his time in prayer. In the sixth year of slavery he had a dream in which he was commanded to return to Britain. Seeing this as a sign, he fled Ireland and subsequently studied in several monasteries in Europe. As Bishop. Patrick was sent by Pope Saint Celestine to evangelize England, then Ireland. In 33 years, he effectively converted Ireland. As a consequence of Patrick's ministry, the monasteries of Ireland were great repositories of learning in Europe during the Dark Ages, and during the Middle Ages, Ireland became known as the Land of Saints.

"If I am worthy, I am ready also to give up my life, without hesitation and most willingly, for Christ's name. I want to spend myself for that country, even in death, if the Lord should grant me this favor."
—*from The Confession of Saint Patrick*

St. Patrick was born 387-390 in Scotland, and died 461-464 in Ireland.

His feast day is March 17, St. Patrick's Day.

Martyrs

St. Agnes

As a young Roman noble raised by a Christian family, Agnes (291-304) made a promise to God to remain pure. But her beauty was such that many men came to her, including the son of a Roman prefect. When she refused his proposal for marriage, she was condemned to death. Roman law did not allow for the execution of virgins; so, according to tradition, her clothing was removed and she was dragged to a brothel. As she prayed while being dragged naked through the streets, her hair grew to such an extent that it covered her body, and those men who tried to molest her were struck blind. She was taken out onto the streets to be burned, but the stakes would not ignite. The officer in charge of her execution used his sword and cut her head from her body.

Agnes is often depicted in art holding a lamb as her name is so close to Latin word *agnus*, meaning lamb. She is one of seven women, excluding the Blessed Virgin, commemorated by name in the "Eucharistic Prayer I", and is the Patron Saint of chastity, gardeners, girls, engaged couples, rape victims, and virgins.

Her feast day is January 21.

http://en.wikipedia.org/wiki/Saint_Agnes
http://www.catholic.org/saints/saint.php?saint_id=106

St. Barbara

St. Barbara lived during the early 3rd century. Held prisoner in a tower by her tyrannical father, she developed a rich prayer life and studied in secret with a Christian priest. To honor the Holy Trinity, St. Barbara added a third window to a building designed by her father (he was away on a long journey). Her conversion to Christianity enraged her father; he brought her before the prefect of the province, who ruled that she be tortured and beheaded. Legend tells that her father wielded the death blow; soon after, he was struck by lightning and his body consumed by flames.

St. Barbara is the Patron Saint of our Franciscan Province. In our window, St. Barbara is holding a chalice; an image of the tower which held her captive is in the background.

Her feast day is December 4.

http://www.catholic.org/saints/saint.php?saint_id=166
http://en.wikipedia.org/wiki/Saint_Barbara
http://en.wikipedia.org/wiki/Saint_Barbara

St. Lucy

Lucy was a young Christian woman who vowed her life to the service of Christ. After rejecting a marriage arranged by her mother, her pagan suitor declared to the Governor of Sicily that Lucy was a Christian. Lucy was sentenced to forced prostitution, but, when the guards arrived to take her away, they could not move her. Instead, the governor ordered her to be killed, and she was tortured and then stabbed to death with a dagger. In art she is often depicted holding a plate with two eyes on it, which comes from a story suggesting that, during torture, the guard gouged her eyes out.

St. Lucy was born in 283, and died in 304.

Her feast day is December 13.

http://en.wik ipedia.org/wiki/St._Lucy
http://www.catholic.org/saints/saint.php?saint_id=75

St. Stephen

But he, filled with the Holy Spirit, looked up intently to heaven and saw the glory of God and Jesus standing at the right hand of God, and he said, "Behold, I see the heavens opened and the Son of Man standing at the right hand of God." But they cried out in a loud voice, covered their ears, and rushed upon him together. They threw him out of the city, and began to stone him. The witnesses laid down their cloaks at the feet of a young man named Saul. As they were stoning Stephen, he called out, "Lord Jesus, receive my spirit." Then he fell to his knees and cried out in a loud voice, "Lord, do not hold this sin against them"; and when he said this, he fell asleep.   —*Acts 7: 55-60*

In our window, St. Stephen is depicted holding stones piled on top of a book.

St. Stephen died c. 34–35.

His feast day is December 26.

St. Lawrence

In August 258, the Roman emperor Valerian condemned to death Pope Sixtus II and all bishops, priests, and deacons. On August 10, 258, Lawrence became the seventh and final deacon to be martyred by Valerian. He was roasted for his martyrdom, as indicated in our window by the iron grate at his lower right-hand side.

St. Lawrence was born in 225, and died August 10, 258.

His feast day is August 10.

St. Maurice

St. Maurice was the leader of the Theban Legion, a group of more than 6,000 men who converted to Christianity together. Following their victory suppressing a revolt in Gaul in 287, Maurice and his men were ordered to sacrifice to gods in thanksgiving. They refused and, by order of the Roman emporor, tho ontiro logion was massacred at Agaunum, Switzerland. He is often depicted as a soldier in full armor.

St. Maurice died in 287.

His feast day is September 22.

Founders & Mystics

St. Benedict of Nursia

St. Benedict is the father of monasticism in the West, and founder of the Benedictines, one of the oldest Orders in the Church. His motto was *Ora et Labora* (Pray and work).

Tradition teaches that St. Benedict lived from 480 to 547, though we cannot be sure that these dates are historically accurate.

Benedict is viewed as a monastic leader, not a scholar. The Rule is the sole known example of Benedict's writing, but it manifests his genius to crystallize the best of the monastic tradition and to pass it on to the European West.[1]

Some monks tried to poison him, but he blessed the cup and rendered it harmless.[2]

St. Benedict is often depicted with a bell, a broken cup and serpent representing poison.[3] In our window he is holding a crosier and the broken cup with a serpent.

His feast day is July 11.

(1) from "The Order of Saint Benedict"
http://www.osb.org/gen/benedict.html

(2) from Saints.SQPN.com
http://saints.sqpn.com/saintb02.htm

(3) from Wikipedia.com
http://en.wikipedia.org/wiki/St._Benedict

St. Dominic

Praedicator fidei
Proclaimer of the faith

According to legend, in 1208 the Virgin Mary presented the rosary to Dominic in the church of Prouille, France. The Holy Rosary has always been a fundamental element of Dominican spirituality.[1]

In 1215, Dominic and six followers were given a house in Toulouse, where he established monastic rules of prayer and penance and received permission from the Bishop to preach thoughout the territory. In December 1216, Pope Honorius III gave Dominic the authority to form an order to be named "The Order of Preachers," known as the Dominican Order.

St. Dominic and St. Francis of Assisi were contemporaries and likely met one another. Members of both the Order of Friars Minor and the Order of Preachers moved beyond the walls of the cloister to bring the Gospel into the world.

St. Dominic died on August 6, 1221.

His feast day is August 8.

[1]Wikipedia
http://en.wikipedia.org/wiki/Dominican_Order#Rosary

St. Ignatius Loyola

omnia ad majorem Dei gloriam
All for the glory of God

Ignatius Loyola was the founder and initial Superior General of the Society of Jesus, known as the Jesuits. He is famous as the gatherer of the Spiritual Exercises and as a talented spiritual director.[1]

As a soldier he received a leg wound. The injury left him partially crippled for life.[2] While recuperating he read religious books. This brought about a conversion, and he began to pray, fast, do penance and works of charity, and dedicate himself to God. After some troubles with the Spanish Inquisition, he decided to study for the priesthood.[3]

St. Ignatius is often depicted with the Eucharist, a cross, book and chasible.[4] In the church window, he is wearing a chasible and holding a book, with his right hand raised as if to offer a blessing.

His feast day is July 31.

[1]Catholic Encyclopedia
http://www.newadvent.org/cathen/07639c.htm

[2]http://saints.sqpn.com/sainti01.htm

[3]Origin of the Society of Jesus, http://www.jesuit.org/
WhoAreJesuits/JesuitHistory/default.aspx

[4]http://en.wikipedia.org/wiki/Ignatius_of_Loyola

St. Theresa of Avila

Theresa was born on March 28, 1515. Her mother died when Theresa was just 15, leaving her and nine siblings. In 1535 she joined the Carmelite Order, where she experienced a severe illness. She never completely recovered. Following her illness, she began to experience visions of a wounded Christ. Reputedly, the visions caused her to believe that Christ was with her, and one vision continued for more than two years. Theresa was a profound mystic who wrote extensively about her spiritual experiences in *The Interior Castle*. Theresa reformed the Carmelite Order and founded the convent of Discalced Carmelite Nuns. She supported St. John of the Cross in his efforts to reform the men's branch of the Carmelite Order. In 1970, she became the first woman to receive the honor of Doctor of the Church, conveyed by the Holy See. She died October 4, 1582.

St. Theresa is often depicted holding a quill, an arrow-pierced heart, or a book.

Her feast day is October 15.

http://en.wikipedia.org/wiki/Teresa_of_%C3%81vila
http://www.ccel.org/t/teresa/
http://www.catholic.org/saints/saint.php?saint_id=208
http://www.sacred-texts.com/chr/tic/index.htm

St. Rose of Lima

Born as Isabel to Spanish immigrants to the New World, Rose was a beautiful girl and devoted daughter. She was also devoted to her vow of chastity, so much so that she used pepper and lye to ruin her complexion so she would not be attractive. St. Rose lived and meditated in a garden, raising vegetables and making embroidered items to sell to support her family and help the other poor. She became a Dominican tertiary in 1606, and was considered both a mystic and a visionary. St. Rose received the Stigmata and suffered from assorted physical and mental ailments. She was the first saint born in the Americas, and was founder of social work in Peru. She had a great devotion to St. Catherine of Siena. Many miracles followed her death. St. Rose is often depicted wearing a crown of roses.

St. Rose of Lima was born on April 20, 1586, and died on August 30, 1617.

Her feast day is August 30.

St. Zita

At age twelve, she became a lifelong domestic servant for a family in Lucca. She often gave her own food, and sometimes her master's, to those poorer than herself, causing her great trouble in the household.

A naturally happy disposition and the teaching of a virtuous mother, aided by Divine grace, developed in the child's soul that sweetness and modesty of character and continual and conscientious application to work which constituted her special virtues. After her death numerous miracles were wrought at her intercession, so that she came to be venerated as a saint in the neighborhood of Lucca.

Because of her life as a domestic, St. Zita is a patron saint for domestic workers and maids, and is often asked to help find lost keys. In our window she is shown holding a set of keys.

St. Zita was born c. 1212 and died on April 27, 1272.

Her feast day is April 27.

Marian Side Altar

Marian Side Altar: Statue of Our Lady of Fatima and Mural of Our Lady of Lourdes

"Je suis l'Immaculée conception."
"I am the Immaculate Conception."

THESE ARE THE WORDS spoken by Mary to 14-year-old Bernadette Soubirous on March 25, 1858.

It is somewhat unusual that a devotion for both of these Marian apparitions would be placed together in one side altar. We are not sure exactly when or how the statue of Our Lady of Fatima was placed here. In 1908, when the church was built, Our Lady of Lourdes was the most recent apparition, and we believe that this is why the mural on the back wall of this area was painted to depict that scene.

The Immaculate Conception is the patroness of the Franciscan Order.

In many countries, the Catholic Church celebrates a Mass in honor of "Our Lady of Lourdes" annually on February 11, which is the anniversary of the first apparition.

Et marula originalis non est in te
There is no original sin in Mary.

Tota pulchra es, Maria
Mary, you are full of beauty.

St. Anthony Side Altar: Statue of St. Anthony

THE IMAGE OF Anthony holding the divine infant is a symbol and model for each of us. The image inspires us to go through life clinging to the wonderful mystery of the humble, self-emptying Christ, who accompanies us as a servant of our humanity and of the world's healing.[1]

St. Anthony is also depicted in a medallion in the Franciscan men section. (See page 108.)

[1] Jack Wintz, O.F.M, "Why St. Anthony Holds the Child Jesus," Saint Anthony Messenger Web site, http://www.americancatholic.org/Messenger/Jun2000/Anthony.asp

Si queris miracua
If you seek miracles.

Aegri surget sani
The sick will arise healed.

St. Anthony
Side Altar

The Choir Loft

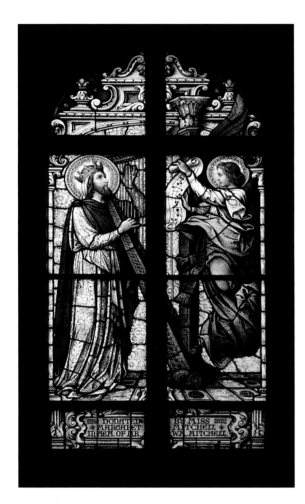

King David

Saul's attendants said to him, "See, an evil spirit from God is tormenting you. Let our lord command his servants here to search for someone who can play the harp. He will play when the evil spirit from God comes upon you and you will feel better." So Saul said to his attendants, "Find someone who plays well and bring him to me." ...Whenever the spirit from God came upon Saul, David would take his harp and play. Then relief would come to Saul; he would feel better, and the evil spirit would leave him.

—1 Samuel 16:15-17;23

St. Cecilia

St. Cecilia lived in third-century Rome and was married to a man she loved, whose name was Valerian. She prayed to saints and angels to guard her virginity and, on her wedding night, told Valerian that her angel protector would prevent consummation of their marriage. Valerian asked to see the angel and was told that would only be possible once he was baptized. So he went to the pope and was baptized.

Returning to Cecilia, he was able to witness the angel, who placed a crown of lilies and roses on both his and Cecilia's heads. Both Valerian and his brother were so moved that they began to bury the bodies of those martyred by the prefect. Soon after, they were arrested and executed. Cecilia was also arrested and condemned to death by suffocation in her own bath house. Locked in the bath for more than a day, Cecilia was unaffected by the heat. Seeing this, the guard in charge made three strikes with his sword in an attempt to decapitate her. But she survived the blows, and the guard left her to bleed to death in the baths. She lived for three days, and is reported to have prayed with those who came to collect her blood.

St. Cecilia is regarded as the patroness of music and is often depicted in art with an organ.

Her feast day is November 22.

Shrines

Statue of Blessed Mother

Mary said:
"My soul proclaims your greatness,
    Oh God,
And my spirit rejoices in you, my Savior.
For you have looked with favor
upon your lowly servant,
and from this day forward
all generations will call me blessed.
For you, the Almighty, have done great
    things for me,
and holy is your Name.
Your mercy reaches from age to age
for those who fear you.
You have shown strength with your arm,
you have scattered the proud in their
    conceit,
you have deposed the mighty from their
    thrones
and raised the lowly to high places.
You have filled the hungry with good
    things,
while you have sent the rich away
    empty.
You have come to the aid of Israel your
    servant,
mindful of your mercy—
the promise you made to our ancestors—
to Sarah and Abraham
and their descendants forever."

—Luke 1: 46-55

Reproduction of Image of Our Lady of Guadalupe

In 1531 a "Lady from Heaven" appeared to Juan Diego, a humble Native American, at Tepeyac, on a hill northwest of what is now Mexico City.

She identified herself as the ever-virgin Holy Mary, Mother of the True God for whom we live, of the Creator of all things, Lord of heaven and the earth.

She made a request for a church to be built on the site, and submitted her wish to the local Bishop. When the Bishop hesitated, and asked her for a sign, the Mother of God obeyed without delay or question to the church's local Bishop, and sent her Native messenger to the top of the hill in mid-December to gather an assortment of roses for the Bishop.

After complying with the Bishop's request for a sign, She also left for us an image of herself imprinted miraculously on the Native's *tilma*, a poor quality cactus-cloth, which should have deteriorated in 20 years but shows no sign of decay 476 years later and still defies all scientific explanations of its origin. It apparently even reflects in Her eyes what was in front of her in 1531.

—*from Our Lady Of Guadalupe Web site*

This is the only image we have of the Holy Mother carrying the baby Jesus in her womb.

Statue of St. Thérèse of Lisieux

"I want to spend my heaven doing good on earth."

—*St. Thérèse of Lisieux*

St. Thérèse of Lisieux lived to be 24 years old. At the age of 16, she entered the Carmelite Order and never left the cloisters. She offered all of her penance and life to increase the love of God. She is the patroness of the Missions. In 1896 she wrote her spiritual memoir, *The Story of a Soul*.

In his apostolic letter of October 19, 1997, Pope John Paul II proclaimed St. Thérèse of Lisieux a Doctor of the Church.

Her feast day is October 1.

Statue of St. Joseph

… An angel of the Lord appeared to him in a dream and said, "Joseph son of David, do not be afraid to take Mary home as your wife, because what is conceived in her is from the Holy Spirit. She will give birth to a son, and you are to give him the name Jesus, because he will save his people from their sins."

—***Matthew 1:20-21***

In the Roman Catholic and other traditions, St. Joseph is the patron saint and protector of the universal Catholic Church, and Patron Saint of workers.[1]

This statue of St. Joseph was in the original St. Francis church building.

His feast days are May 1 for St. Joseph the Worker and March 19 for Joseph, the husband of Mary.

[1] Wikipedia http://en.wikipedia.org/wiki/Saint_Joseph

Statue of St. Maria Goretti

St. Maria was born in 1890 into a poor farming family that eventually lost their farm. Maria's father died from malaria. At the age of eleven, she was attacked by a 19-year-old farm hand. Maria resisted, exclaiming that she would rather die than submit. He stabbed her 14 times. From her hospital bed, Maria forgave the young man and asked God to forgive him. Captured and imprisoned, he had a vision of a young girl picking lilies and offering them to him. As he accepted them, each lily burst into a white flame. He experienced a conversion as a result and repented. He testified at Maria's cause for beatification and, when she was declared a saint by Pope Pius XII in 1950, he was in St. Peter's Square. She was canonized for her purity—the youngest person ever recognized as a saint by the Church.

Her feast day is July 6.

http://saints.sqpn.com/saintm09.htm
http://www.mariagoretti.org/mariabio.htm
http://www.catholic.org/saints/saint.
php?saint_id=78

Go in peace to love and serve the Lord.

Thanks be to God

WE ADORE YOU most holy Lord Jesus Christ,

here, and in all your churches throughout the world;

and we bless you,

because by your holy cross,

you have redeemed the world.

Additional Sources

PASSAGES FROM SCRIPTURE have been quoted from several translations:

New American Bible (NAB) Copyright © 1991, 1986, 1970 Confraternity of Christian Doctrine, Inc., Washington, DC. All rights reserved.

New International Version (NIV) Copyright © 1973, 1978, 1984 by International Bible Society

New American Standard Bible (NASB) Copyright © 1960, 1962, 1963, 1968, 1971, 1972, 1973, 1975, 1977, 1995 by The Lockman Foundation

The Inclusive New Testament Copyright ©1996 Priests for Equality

The following Web sites have been used as sources for much of the material in this book. We encourage the reader to explore them in greater depth.

The Catholic Encyclopedia New Advent - *http://www.newadvent.org/cathen/index.html*
Catholic Online - *http://www.catholic.org/encyclopedia*

Wikipedia - *http://en.wikipedia.org/wiki/Main_Page*

Star Quest Production Network, Saints Online - *http://saints.sqpn.com/*

Catholicity - *http://www.catholicity.com/*

The Sacred Heart Province (Archive) – *http://www.thefriars.org/archives/items/adrian.htm*

American Catholic - *http://www.americancatholic.org/*

The Catechism of the Catholic Church - *http://www.vatican.va/archive/ccc/index.htm*

The Vatican Web site - *http://www.vatican.va/phome_en.htm*

The United States Conference of Catholic Bishops Web site - *http://www.nccbuscc.org/*

Tirol Glass Company Web site - *http://cgi.thewebproduction.com/tirolerglasmalerei/_new/site*

Adoro Te Devote

1. Godhead here in hiding, whom I do adore,
Masked by these bare shadows, shape and nothing more,
See, Lord, at thy service low lies here a heart
Lost, all lost in wonder at the God thou art.

2. Seeing, touching, tasting are in thee deceived:
How says trusty hearing? That shall be believed;
What God's Son has told me, take for truth I do;
Truth himself speaks truly or there's nothing true.

3. On the cross thy godhead made no sign to men,
Here thy very manhood steals from human ken:
Both are my confession, both are my belief,
And I pray the prayer of the dying thief.

4. I am not like Thomas, wounds I cannot see,
But can plainly call thee Lord and God as he;
Let me to a deeper faith daily nearer move,
Daily make me harder hope and dearer love.

5. O thou our reminder of Christ crucified,
Living Bread, the life of us for whom he died,
Lend this life to me then: feed and feast my mind,
There be thou the sweetness man was meant to find.

6. Bring the tender tale true of the Pelican;
Bathe me, Jesu Lord, in what thy bosom ran—
Blood whereof a single drop has power to win
All the world forgiveness of its world of sin.

7. Jesu, whom I look at shrouded here below,
I beseech thee send me what I thirst for so,
Some day to gaze on thee face to face in light
And be blest for ever with thy glory's sight.
Amen.

1. Adoro te devote, latens Deitas,
Quae sub his figuris vere latitas;
Tibi se cor meum totum subiicit,
Quia te contemplans, totum deficit.

2. Visus, tactus, gustus in te fallitur,
Sed auditu solo tuto creditur;
Credo quidquid dixit Dei Filius,
Nil hoc verbo veritatis verius.

3. In Cruce latebat sola Deitas.
At hic latet simul et humanitas:
Ambo tamen credens, atque confitens,
Peto quod petivit latro paenitens.

4. Plagas, sicut Thomas, non intueor,
Deum tamen meum te confiteor:
Fac me tibi semper magis credere,
In te spem habere, te diligere.

5. O memoriale mortis Domini,
Panis vivus vitam praestans homini:
Praesta meae menti de te vivere,
Et te illi semper dulce sapere.

6. Pie pellicane Iesu Domine,
Me immundum munda tuo Sanguine:
Cuius una stilla salvum facere
Totum mundum quit ab omni scelere.

7. Iesu, quem velatum nunc aspicio,
Oro, fiat illud, quod tam sitio,
Ut te revelata cernens facie,
Visu sim beatus tuae gloriae.
Amen.

St. Francis Pastors

1895-1896	Augustine McClory, O.F.M.
1896-1900	Titus Hugger, O.F.M.
Feb-Sept 1900	Pius Nierman, O.F.M.
1900-1904	Godfrey Heolters, O.F.M.
1904-1906	Victor Aertker, O.F.M.
1906-1912	Godfrey Hoelters, O.F.M.
1912-1914	Felix Raab, O.F.M.
1914-1917	Apollinaris Johmann, O.F.M.
1917-1922	Humilis Wiese, O.F.M.
1922-1923	Felix Raab, O.F.M.
1923-1924	Ildephonse Moser, O.F.M.
1924-1928	Solanus Crowley, O.F.M.
1928-1931	Clement Berberich, O.F.M.
1931-1937	Samuel Goggin, O.F.M.
1937-1943	Gregory Wooler, O.F.M.
1943-1946	Gilbert Zlatar, O.F.M.
1946-1958	Ike Powleson, O.F.M.
1958-1961	Harold Moran, O.F.M.
1961-1967	Giles Valcovich, O.F.M.
1967-1968	Basil Kelley, O.F.M.
1968-1969	Gratian Gabel, O.F.M.
1969	Ernest Wilson, O.F.M.
1969-1976	John Vaughn, O.F.M.
1976-1977	Claude Riffel, O.F.M.
1977-1978	Enrique Parisi, O.F.M.
1978-1982	Herb Wheatley, O.F.M.
1982-1988	Mel Bucher, O.F.M.
1988-1995	Barry Brunsman, O.F.M.
1995-1999	Richard Juzix, O.F.M.
1999	Michael Harvey, O.F.M., Administrator
1999-2002	Ken Laverone, O.F.M.
2002-2003	Micah Muhlen, O.F.M.
Jan-May 2003	Michel Gagnon, O.F.M.
2003-	Anthony M. Garibaldi, O.F.M.